ISBN-10: 0615882935

ISBN-13: 978-0615882932 (KC Rhoads)

BORED TO SLEEP

TRYPTOPHAN FOR THE INSOMNIAC

Printed in U.S.A.

www.kcrhoads.com

Email: authorkc@kcrhoads.com

http://www.kcrhoads.com/home2/kcrhoads/public
 _html/

Bored To Sleep

Bored To Sleep: Trytophan for the Insomniac

Bored To Sleep

Prologue

If you are an insomniac, such as me, then you will appreciate this book meant to distract, react, and possibly even "bore you to sleep!"

This book may be exactly what you need when you find your mind wandering in 100 different directions.

Often, I want to read something short and simple; guaranteed to put me to sleep.

What I don't want to do is pick up a novel, find myself unable to put it down, and then not even have the slightest bit of rest for the night. Each chapter is self-contained.

Sleep…..ah, I am so tired, the bed looks inviting, and I just KNOW I am going to fall asleep.

As I crawl into bed, it begins…….thoughts begin swirling through my head. I tell myself "What a luxury to lay here and finally filter the day's events." This is when I do my best thinking.

Why don't I just purchase a tape recorder and dictate a to-do list for the next workday, or jot down notes on a pad or in my phone so I can put it out of my mind? Perhaps, a glass of warm milk (yuck), herbal tea, or a game of solitaire on the computer will do the trick.

No, I'm too tired and if I just close my eyes, sleep will come.

But wait! It's so amazing to have time to revel in these thoughts and solve the world's problems.

I start with child#1 and work my way through child#4. Frustration moves in I can't solve their problems and now I'm worried!

Okay, let me think about what I can put on my task list for tomorrow. I prioritize in my mind, thinking that will rest my angst and sleep will come. Not!

My mind races on and on with the dos, don'ts, the what-ifs, and the happy places.

This book will give you chapters of my meandering journey, put voice to how silly it all seems, and quite frankly, make you vow to only read one chapter at a time, and promptly fall asleep!

If you share this in common with me, then I think this is the book for you. Short, sweet, and meaningless!

Bored To Sleep

I love to bore people, so hold onto your hats, our journey is about to begin. A journey to nowhere, but fun nonetheless!

Chapter 1. Cyber-Granny

This one may entertain more than tire you, but use this to remove the reason you are still awake and read about Grandma.

My grandma was having an affair with the mailman! He wore yellow, looked as if he was running and always in the same direction. Whenever he left mail, the mailbox flag would be raised.

It was 1997 and the pressure was on to get email. I couldn't freaking believe it: my own 80 year old grandmother had email before me!

She coined herself the cyber-granny and her AOL username, BLARO, was the first initial of her last name followed by her Christian name spelled backwards. Her name was Oral and originally she used that as her screen name. You should have seen the family trying to convince her that she couldn't very well put "Oral" out into cyber-space. And this was before it was known that perverts were stalking users. She tried our patience in those days. We kept saying, "Common sense, Grandma, common sense! Isn't that what you have always preached to us?"

Cyber-granny looked at us and laughed heartily. She was five feet nothing and just as wide as she was tall. Who, she stated, was going to make sexual innuendoes at a lady with her girth?

"Grandma, they don't see you; they see your screen name and what you describe on your profile page." (This was before photos were everywhere online.) At that time, users selected a photo from their physical photo albums. Photo in hand the search would begin for a friend with a scanner so a file could be made. Creating a file was beyond the skill level of most email consumers. Many users still did not even use digital cameras. Hence, not many emailers out there had pictures on-line! Everything was open to the imagination. (I did know one girl back then who found a photo of an unbecoming man. She figured out how to place that photo of him on her email profile when she needed to discourage a too ardent pursuer). There were many frauds back in those days, but I digress.

Naiveté was rampant among email users. It was a whole new world; especially for one little old lady who hated to get out and drive. Email was just her ticket to an easily accessible social life.

Back to the profile page. Do you remember those? Grandma had AOL as her internet service provider. When a user signed up for an account, they could tell a little bit about themselves on a profile tab. Items such as marital status, hobbies, age, and quotes were commonplace. It wasn't abnormal to see quotes about world peace, or "whirled peas" as the old circulated joke used to go, or comments such as "I love my family", or "looking for a relationship."

But not for Oral: she had to write quotes such as "I want to donate my body to science" and "sex is overrated." "If God meant breasts to be used for sex, then why did He make hot pepper for my nipples?" "If I were born in the 60's I'd smoke marijuana and join a nudist colony."

Grandma's interests were "Studying the human body, science, reading, and meeting people." And far be it from Grandma to tell her age: that field was left blank!

AOL had all kinds of cool features. An AOL user could type in certain key words to find out who was online at that particular moment. AOL would match the description they typed with keywords in user profiles. In Grandma's case, if someone typed in "sex" AND "oral", well, needless to say her inbox would fill up.

Now this did annoy her and conversely, the thought of returning so many emails was daunting to her, not to mention how disgusted she was by the sexual content.

She had bursitis and it hurt to hold her arm up for too long. Typing was a chore. Finally this convinced Grandma to change her screen name to BLARO: fewer emails, and less trashy talk.

Still not deterred, Grandma thought she should have instant messenger running, too. Instant messenger was the best way to get pinged by other users online at the same time you were on email. If your profile interested them, a simple message typed by that party would pop up in a separate window over your email.

Rapidly, conversations between strangers could emerge. Grandma decided these strangers were becoming too disgusting! She hated sex and it seemed sex remained the topic of the day.

Our next lesson for Grandma was to teach her how to "toss" someone. In AOL world if a user was harassing you, they could be reported to AOL so the spammer could be blocked from your email. It was called "tossing". Sometimes users did not appreciate being "tossed" and they would come skulking back once the prerequisite amount of time had passed and AOL returned their online privileges.

Grandma would receive such dire warnings as "I see you" and "watch your back." She decided it was time to be proactive. She would no longer instant message with strangers, but only with family. Since she wanted her conversations with us to remain uninterrupted, she learned how to invite us to a chat room. Her profile quotes eliminated words such as sex, oral, nude, and marijuana. The chat room was given a name and by unanimous vote Grandma wasn't allowed to name it.

Grandma was getting savvy, but her bursitis was getting worse. She had heard from the occupational therapist that there was a thing called voice recognition for computers. If she could get the computer to type for her, then she could be on the computer even longer. Polite society dictated that if mail was received, it should be answered, and in Grandma's world that bled over into internet mail. By then her love of all things cyber had spread to the remainder of her family and younger friends. We were all on AOL email now and we faithfully emailed her.

Once we struggled our way through the early versions of voice activated software, Grandma found her eyes were failing her. She was unable to stare at her screen for hours on end. Grandma's 13" monitor clearly was not large enough for her aging eyes. It seemed Grandma's needs were mounting as rapidly as the cyber world changed.

Our family sent emails out to each other asking everyone to pitch in, and we surprised Grandma with a large monitor. Her days were set! She could peruse her computer for longer periods of time, much to my grandfather's chagrin. (His hobby was collecting newspapers, clipping out articles of interest, and pasting them into notebooks: He managed to fill an entire room with notebooks by the time he died). To keep him out of Grandma's hair, we all mailed him newspapers and magazines from across the country. To Grandpa's way of thinking, that computer crap that his wife engaged in was just plain ludicrous!

I like to think my grandmother was one of the pioneers. Our aging citizens have been given many more opportunities to exercise their minds and interact with all manner of people. I know in cyber-granny's case, she looked forward to opening her computer each and every morning.

Grandma only got to use the computer for 4 short years before she passed. One of the last things she heard in her little apartment on the day of her stroke was, "You've got Mail"!

At this point you should be smiling and carefree. Sleep my friend, sleep!

Chapter 2: Max the Slovak Ghost

Oh, this is a good one!

Relaxation….somehow after another hour, I nod off again. It's so real, the conversation is fascinating……I meet Max.

Did I tell you I'm into home décor? I'll save that for another chapter, but perhaps it'll help you understand I'm not totally crazy when I introduce this dream.

One night when I managed to drift off, I ended up in an old house. The house itself was located somewhere in the Midwest where all old houses are, in my dreams, and was built in the 1890's.

Throughout the house were your typical old farmhouse type items: an apron front white sink in the kitchen, a skirted curtain running across the front of the cupboard below, a claw-foot tub in the only bathroom, and musty smelling wallpaper on the walls.

A bit like Goldie Locks and the Three Bears, I made my way up a creaking, narrow wood staircase. At the top of the stairs and to the right was a small 11' x 10 'room, again with the peeling wallpaper, but an inviting featherbed onto which I promptly plop. (I'm always tired).

Curiously I looked around the room to see what else was there: a single bulb suspended from the ceiling, lending eerie shadows to the walls. Opposite from the bed was a single small washstand with a pitcher and bowl, a vanity-type mirror attached on 2 spindles.

Next to the bed there was a nightstand. Here's where the dream is weird, as are all my dreams. The nightstand was located to the left of the bed. It had patchy avocado green paint on it, and there were 4 drawers total. The top row was divided right down the middle with 2 equal sized drawers, each with a round knob in the center of them. The middle and bottom drawers were the width of the stand. There was a knob handle on the middle row, and two horizontal handles on the bottom drawer. All of the handles were painted red wood. (What is it about me and painted red wood?)

If you think about this, the nightstand knobs took on the appearance of a face. The top 2 knobs on the smaller drawers were the eyes, the middle knob, the nose, and the 2 horizontal handles the mouth.

Hilariously, yet ever so normally in my dream, the nightstand introduced himself to me as I lay on the feather bed. With each phrase, the bottom drawer would slide in and out as if in rhythm to the words.

"Hi, I'm Max, the Slovak Ghost. Would you like to know where I (the nightstand) came from?" Of course, I answered "yes", since I was passionate about all old pieces of furniture. Max proceeded to explain that he had once been painted a bright lemon yellow and that he came from the country of……………………..DARN IT! I'm awake again. A Slovak ghost? I have to write this one down! Who comes up with these things? Max? Huh?

Shoot, now what? I need to fall back asleep, but I can't stop wondering where that dream came from! I swear, some of the dreams I have would sell as Sci-Fi blockbusters, because the graphics are so amazing. Even stranger, I don't like sci-fi, but I sure can dream in 3D. The human brain is such a great thing.

What is the human brain, anyway; is it 2 hemispheres? Is it gooey like intestines, or hard like muscle, or wait, it is muscle, right? Don't people tell you to exercise your brain; it'll keep dementia at bay? Is that true?

Heck, my in-laws could prove that theory. My father n law lived to be 94 and he did crossword puzzles every day until he fell and broke his hip. Yep, you got it: he was dreaming and while dreaming he began thrashing around and threw himself right out of bed....the beginning of the end.

I digress......my mother-n-law, still with us at 96, does crossword puzzles every single day as published in the Sacramento Bee. The only time her mind had not been sharp was when she was hospitalized and without her newspaper. A coincidence? I don't know...anesthesia side effects were probably more like it.

Talk about making people weird, that's anesthesia. My father-n-law used to swear he was being tortured at the hospital and all the while it was the Demerol speaking. Then, throw in the family member who believed his dad really was being tortured, because he was so convincing. The concerned family member then proceeded to chew out the hospital staff.

Don't you feel sorry for the hospital nurses? People are affected by their illnesses or medications, they believe it to be real, they're not happy about the feeling, or for that matter being in the hospital, so they take it out on the staff.

I wonder if staff at hospital and nursing homes wish they could sedate the patients at will? What do they do? They dial up the on-call doctor suggesting that perhaps the patient in bed A would rest better if they had a mild sedative. But they forget: the sedative is going to make them even loopier: it is a never ending cycle. I know, maybe they should sedate the demanding relative! Or, the nurse who desperately needs one after the on-call doctor rips her a new one for calling him in the middle of the night! Again, I'm off....where was I? What was I dreaming? Can I return to my dream? Night, night, night, .ah yes! Night Stand!

Chapter 3: Was that a Table Saw?

Tonight I am relaxed, soothed, calmed by the mindless television I watched before bed. My mind has been emptied of the day's craziness and sweet slumber is upon me. As I'm dreaming, I am quite annoyed that the neighbor's table saw is drilling away in the middle of the night. Why in the world, I wonder, would they be so thoughtless? As I lay in bed, the droning of the saw takes on a cadence, and it blends into the background, much as any oft repeated noise.

The saw represents construction, and a beautifully crafted built-in bookcase emerges as a fireplace surround. It is a satisfying feeling to have accomplished such a piece of skilled workmanship. The saw is now my friend.

Suddenly, there is a clap of thunder! The abruptness startles me. I hear a sound following the thunder that resembles someone squirting two sudden puffs of inhaler into their lungs: more thunder, more inhaler, and then a whistling teapot. What in the world is going on? Where did my beautiful cabinet go?

Bored To Sleep

I am startled into wakefulness (once again), and see that the thunder is none other than my husband's snoring! I want to throttle him! This is even worse than the neighbor's ill manners! Roll over, I say! Obligingly, he does as I request.

Why me? Why do I have to hear snoring on the one night I was going to sleep? How long was this snoring going on since it blended right in with my dreams? Is it going to be necessary to dream around his snoring? I fixate on the word snoring.

What causes snoring, I ask?

Snoring can be caused by sleep apnea. Sleep apnea is also known as OSA, Obstructive Sleep Apnea. When the sleeper's throat relaxes, the tissues within the throat can vibrate, making all those strange noises in my dream. Of course this is not a medical journal by any means; the explanation is simply meant to bore you silly!

If you're like me, you've probably heard about remedies for snore sufferers, such as turning on their side, losing weight, not drinking alcohol, or the best one; the C-PAP (Continuous Positive Airway Pressure) machine.

Have you seen these machines? My husband has one, but certainly was not wearing it that night. It gives my spouse an undeniably unsexy appearance. Yes, it has been compared to Darth Vader, but not a desirable Darth. The machine has a mask that goes over the entire nose and mouth, with a rubber tube connected to a square 8" x 6" machine that pushes air into the users' system, coupled with moisture from a built-in humidifier.

My husband must wear a Band-Aid across the bridge of his nose to prevent the mask from chafing: a band-aided, strapped, hosed Darth Vader.......forced to sleep on his back so the apparatus remains in place. Which is the lesser of two evils? A new noise to deal with: the machine? It goes full circle, snoring, dreaming of the machine, and me still saying, "Put on your mask", as I elbow the poor man to wake up! At least this droning will be constant, predictable, and at an acceptable noise decibel.

Chapter 4: The Sewing fanatic

As a child, I thought the most boring place on planet earth was the fabric store. My mother prided herself on being a champion seamstress. She could sew anything in any style, shape, color, texture, or length. In fact, I was certain that she invented the blue polyester leisure suit, which my dad obligingly wore. Should I save that for another chapter: public humiliation?

In order to be such a fabulous seamstress, one must indulge in the purchase of fabrics, patterns, notions such as zippers, buttons, elastic, and anything else necessary to assemble the perfect creation.

My heart would sink to the bottom of my toes when we entered the fabric store. I kid you not; there are aisles and aisles and AISLES of fabrics. The fabrics are wrapped around a cardboard form called a bolt, which labels the fabric with how many inches wide it is (usually 45" or 60"), whether it's cotton, nylon, polyester, wool, or silk, and how much per yard the fabric costs.

If that was all there was in the selection of a new garment, it would not have been so bad, but these trips could take up to three hours at a time. It is the pattern drawers that did me in. A pattern is an envelope approximately 8" x 6" with tissue paper inserted outlining various pieces, which all together, make the let's say, dress. The patterns are first viewed in sewing Catalogs such as Simplicity, Vogue, or Butterick. Each catalog is divided into sections: boys, girls, toddlers, babies, adult women, adult men, and then subsections of each: casual wear, slacks, skirts, dresses, blouses, pajamas, and accessories. Within each subsection are sizes which are listed according to measurements of bust, chest, waist, hips, and sleeve length. I think I was the only kid in school who always knew her measurements. Honestly, I still remember my 8th grade hip measurement and I was devastated when it was a curvy number.

After the patterns are viewed and the desired outfit selected, a corresponding number on that pattern picture is written on a scratch piece of paper, much as you would scribble when utilizing the library card catalog. There are now several shorter aisles housing the large bulky horizontal file cabinets containing the said patterns. The file cabinets are sorted by Simplicity, Vogue, Butterick, and then by pattern number. The one my mom always seemed to want was in the bottom drawer: there she would be on the floor sifting through the numbers.

At last! The outfit now matches patterns of a dress, blazer and another pattern of a jacket. We move onto fabric selection. On the back of the pattern, there are suggested fabric types for the blazer. It should be velour, or medium weight wool. So, we trudge over to the aisle for velour. There are at least 3 dozen types of velour in various colors, designs, and nap. Oh yes, nap is the direction the grain of the fabric runs and it can be a low nap which means thin, or a higher nap, which is thick: think of shag carpet that is long or short. A long drawn out process then ensues about what color, will the cat hair show, do we want plain on the blazer and plaid on the pants, or plaid on the blazer and plain on the pants? Once decided, we again consult the back of the pattern envelope to determine how many yards of this bolt of fabric we need. I talk her out of the dress. A small victory!

My feet are beginning to hurt: I'm an impatient, tired, bored, and hungry kid. But alas, we are not finished. We read the pattern envelope for the pants: seersucker, it suggests. What is seersucker? From what I recall, seersucker is a kind of cotton and it's sort of puckery. The seersucker aisle sports even more selections and I'm horrified to see that my mom has determined that my pants will be in plaid seersucker. Can it get any worse? Don't ask!

We go through the rest of the selection process much as before.

Now we must wait in line at the cutting table where a kindly attendant cuts according to how many yards we determined were required for each bolt of fabric. Once armed with the fabric, I turn toward the check-out.

I am crushed to find out that now we must select notions. Yep, the back of the pattern envelope tells us we need 2 spools of cotton polyester thread, 1 yard of 2" wide elastic (you guessed it, the dreaded elastic waistband), 3 brass buttons for the blazer, 1 smaller button to decorate the elastic-waist pants, and interface. Interface, in case you're wondering, is a stiff material that can be ironed on the inside edge of waistbands, collars, cuffs, and anything else you want to make firm. (You people and your minds in the gutter..... Stay with me here.)

Do you have any idea how long it takes to choose these notions? We must hold up the spools of thread to the fabrics for the perfect match, as we do the buttons. The zipper must match the fabric and the thread. Did you know zippers can be cotton or polyester, visible or invisible?

I elbow my sister hard and whisper, "Do not dare ask where your outfit is!" Can you imagine going through all of that again? It doesn't matter; my mother already determined she was next. I imagine myself in a happy place, far far away. And happy it becomes, as my mother determines we will wait until next payday to outfit my sister and select my dress.

Oh, and one last point: I now love the fabric store and get immense pleasure in wandering around it at will, fingering the various fabrics and perusing the books. There is one huge difference: I go solo and I'm fast!

Chapter 5: The Polyester Leisure Suit

Let me preface this story with the fact that not only did my mom make my dad a powder blue leisure suit, he also had to model it in a local fashion show, along with my mom in her matching blue polyester pantsuit. Hand over heart; I cannot make this stuff up

To make matters worse, we lived in a small town: a population of 1200. Yes, we knew pretty much everyone. This little town had a high school, populated by 4 surrounding communities; so everyone knew me, then age 16. My mom talked me into modeling a dress that I made. Now I am not only an innocent by-stander, but an unwilling participant: guilty by association!

My father had no clue how ridiculous he looked, so he willingly supported my mother in this endeavor. To add to the excitement, my mother's favorite gospel singer happened to be visiting an affluent couple in our town. His name was George Beverly Shea. My mom studied voice for 7 years (another chapter), and was just gob-smacked that he was there to see her model, while crushed that she did not volunteer to sing prior to the show.

To help, I will paint a nice picture for you to meditate upon as you fall asleep. Following, will be a detailed description of their outfits and the walk down the aisle. (George Beverly Shea was in the front row, by the way!)

My mom color coordinated everything. She and my dad were assigned to walk down the aisle together so EVERYONE could take a gander at their matching gear.

Mom was wearing powder blue polyester pants. They were hard-waisted, zip-front (polyester zipper) fly pants. The style is stove pipe. Stove pipe pants were popular in the 70's. They were not bell bottoms, nor were they form fitting straight legged pants. Stove pipe pants were snug in the rear (and my mom had a LARGE derriere), with straight lined, but loose fitting legs. The legs of the pants were the same width from the upper thigh to the ankle. Now remember, my mom had a large behind, she did NOT work out, and the fabric was polyester. Are you still awake and following me here? Can anyone say jello and dimples?

Her blouse also was polyester. The background was striped horizontally with 2" wide navy, pale blue, white, and yellow stripes. To my horror, she wore this tucked in.

Over the blouse, she made a short sleeved jacket, matching the fabric of her pants. It was a box type shape, came to mid-hip (the dimples were not hidden), and had a nice row of double stitching around the sleeve and jacket hems. It was button front with non-descript pale blue buttons.

To complete this ensemble, she wore white buckle side sandals with a low 1" heel. Since it was prior to Labor Day, the white sandals didn't add to my dismay. Maybe you've heard the saying "no white shoes before Memorial Day or after Labor Day."

Arm in arm with my mom was my father in his leisure suit. The slacks and the blazer matched my mother's, except, fortunately, his jacket had long sleeves. His shirt was identical to hers. It resembled an early version of the polo shirt. His shirt was also tucked in, with the blazer open.

The crowning glory for my dad's ensemble was that he wore his black lace up mailman shoes and horror of horrors: the dreaded white socks.

As they appear in the curtains, an MC announces that this is Gene and Carol. She made sure everyone in the audience was aware that the fashions they saw were the brainchild of Carol.

Mom and Dad made it to the runway, and then they pivoted to return to the curtain. My mom's behind in those polyester slacks looked like two large turtles in a sack. I was embarrassed for her and myself. Video cameras had not been invented: there was no way for her to know that polyester was not her friend.

It was now my turn to go backstage and prepare to show off my dress. I told myself, all is well: maybe my classmates did not realize that was my mom and dad out there. I heard the MC announce, "And next is KC, daughter to Carol and Gene, whom you just witnessed in their leisure wear."

Well, it sure appeared the apple didn't fall far from the tree, as I also had discovered our newer variety of polyester, when selecting this simply beautiful nylon polyester dress. We thought this dress would be all the rage, as it hung so silkily from a high bodice and moved with my body. "Oh no, does this mean I must swagger? Do I have turtles, too?" No, I feel better: she said I have a high bodice! Most of my humiliation stemmed from being 16. At that age there was nothing more mortifying than the fact that my mom and dad modeled together in public. The dimples and turtles in the sack probably went unnoticed by all but me! Perhaps that's a bit optimistic, but......

On top of everything else, my parents had their adored first grandchild; a girl. Not to be outdone, my mom thought it was appropriate to also make my niece a little dress with a matching jacket and bonnet. The dress, jacket, and bonnet were in the same pale blue as their polyester leisure suits. Thankfully, the dress was in blue-checked gingham and all of it was out of stiff cotton. However, the rim of that bonnet was huge: my little niece would not see daylight in that thing! It was hideous, yet at 10 months versus my 16 years, she could have cared less! I learned that fashion shows were all in one's perspective of how people perceive you. You either care, or you dismiss it. I had a lesson that day from my niece. When doing something new, smile through it, because it's going to take place anyway.

I like to tie things up in happy endings, so you can close this chapter and go to bed smiling. If you have a teenager, you have probably lost your "cool", but the good news is, you can stop stressing about it; your cool never comes back!

The next chapter is about how my mom lost her cool with my sister and me.

Chapter 6: The voice lessons

By the time this chapter is complete, you will be able to recite the vowels necessary to warm up your vocal chords. They are O, EE, AH, EE, OOH. Additionally, you will learn my version of what a chord and a scale is. One last tool needed if you desire to reenact said voice lessons will be a cake spatula.

A cake spatula must be stainless steel, with a good reflective spreading blade (meant for frosting) at least 8" long. It should have a 4" solid handle out of wood or hard plastic, so the singer can have a strong grip. They even have spatula grips for arthritis sufferers. Spatulas were plentiful so my sister and I knew we could not make the spatula disappear.

How, you may ask, does one become interested in studying voice, outside of school or college? In my mother's case, she had two young daughters, age 7 and 9. In our Midwest town, the majority of families went to church. Before we moved to the town of 1200 people, we lived in a city of about 100,000 people, with a river dividing the West side from the East side. We lived on the West side, but attended a large church on the East side, as did the rest of my dad's family. After the voice lessons, the people on the East side of the river were probably happy to keep Mom and her vocal practice on the West side and out of earshot! The drive across the river also gave my mom the time to warm-up her vocals.

The church staff had a pastor and a youth pastor, who would also double as the music director. Everyone else volunteered their positions, such as organist, pianist, Sunday school teachers, ushers, and janitors. The difficult task had been to find a youth pastor who could also sing.

One day, the church hit pay dirt. They found a man named Wesley who wanted to move his family down from Canada. He was a mysterious, gorgeous foreigner, with an equally gorgeous family. He just so happened to have 3 sons all around our ages. Do you know that family smelled good? They had a family scent that should have been bottled. I could go off on quite a tiresome tangent about that smell and how it affected me at such a tender age. Wesley's son, Mark, will forever be imbedded in my memory when I smell that musky, clean, downy smell all mixed together. It's a great trigger.

Bored To Sleep

Okay, I am reigning myself in and getting back to the voice lessons. Rev. Wesley came to our church and sang a solo. It made even my 7 year old knees weak, as it was a deep rich baritone, with excellent control. I felt as if he had stepped out of an opera and onto our podium. He was hired! His idea of youth group was to create youth choirs from age 6 all the way to high school/college age. Additionally, he directed the adult choir, joined by both my mother and father. The music he could inspire and create was heavenly. Life centered on music.

Now my mom was a regular for the Sunday morning or evening special music performances. Additionally, she was on the call list for local funeral homes when the bereft family members needed a singer. She loved to sing in a high soprano voice. My paternal grandma also went to our church. In her mind's eye, no one was good enough for my dad, and she pecked at my mother like the media would tear up a star: my mother never measured up. When my mother found out that Rev. Wesley was giving voice lessons, she urged my dad to let her try. Surely this would impress her mother in law.

The fun began. Mother took these voice lessons very seriously, or should I say ser-ee-o-ous-lee. Oh EE Ah EE Ooh EE Ah EE Oh. We heard this in the scale format on every car ride. Mother's metal spatula would be held horizontally under her nose as she continued to vocalize with Oh EE Ah EE Ooh EE Ah EE Oh up and down a 5 note scale. A scale in music is a series of notes that run in steps up and down, melodically. A full scale has 8 notes: they are c, d,e,f,g,a,b, c. In the case of her vowels, they were to the tune of c d e f g and then back down g f e d c. (This is good; I can feel I am losing you in this wearisome explanation of scales and the ooh ee ahs). Each time she descended the scale, it went up a step, so the next ooh ee aahs would be a bit higher because she started at the note d and went like this d e f g a g f e d. Ironic: it spells def gag fed. Somehow when you're tired, that seems hilarious!

One of her favorite car rides to practice scales and enunciation was when we had a 3 hour drive to my grandparent's farm in Wisconsin. The dog, my sister, and I would be packed into the backseat, my dad driving, and my mom making steam with her spatula. Of course my sister and I had to sing along: this is like a comedian being fed the straight line not to be passed up. Her feelings would get hurt as we operatically sang her scales. She would shriek at us to stop making fun of her: that was when we definitely knew she was not cool. The vocalizing, the shrieking, and the repetitiveness of it all seemed so old-fashioned. The shrieking should have been enough to warm her vocal cords up. But just remember, things that drove you crazy as a kid will later make warm memories. My sister and I still laugh over those car rides and the reactions we could get out of her.

When we were not in the car, Mother would lie on her back on the floor and sing up into her spatula to practice breathing from her diaphragm. If she could steam it while lying down, all was ready.

Mind you, she did this for 7 years, so it is ingrained in my psyche. No, Wheel of Fortune, I do not wish to buy a vowel! I've had enough, thank you. Not only did I get to listen to these exercises but I was also accomplished at the piano by then, so Mother elected me to be her personal pianist. Now that is a fun childhood. Humdrum for sure! It was fun to tease her, though, and tell her she was a little pitchy: too sharp. Yes, passive aggressive.

Slowly, my mother's solos took on a broader, deeper, more vibrato tone. She was the star pupil and her practicing paid off. She wasn't singing in Italian yet, but it was probably next. And can you believe it? My paternal grandma still hated her singing. Now she bemoaned the days when her daughter in law could croon and not be so vibratory. My grandma would say her voice had been just fine before and that she just wasted my dad's money for all those silly lessons.

My little mom was not going to please her mother in law to save her life. After I began to grow up I counseled her to quit trying. Isn't it the son's obligation to his wife to make her acceptable to his mother and have her back at all costs? Do you men do that? If you do, your wife will be very grateful, wink wink! OK, this is where the men check out and fall asleep and the women decide voice lessons are not for them.

When I grew up, I was certain I would not be a singer. Who could compete with an opera singer mom? I did keep up piano and accompanied choirs but very few singing parts came my way. I decided to go into the medical field. I wanted to be a missionary nurse in France, although at that time, I never thought to ask France if my services were needed, which they were not. What's a girl supposed to do?

I was smart: straight A's and personable, so why not learn the medical business. Oh it was such an easy thing to do as I got sucked into this strange new world.

Chapter 7. The Medical Office

In my 20's, I innocently applied for a job in a Plastic Reconstructive Hand Surgeon's office. There was an older woman named Ruth who was going to teach me everything I needed to know. She would leave those little 1"x 2" sticky notes all over the desk to remind me to say this or that on the phone, get the patients insurance card, collect their fee, type up their claim form while they were in the back with the doctor, slip the form out of the typewriter by the time the patient came out of the exam room, have them sign it, and then mail it to obtain reimbursement. That was the easy part. Each part of the job had a corresponding sticky note.

As time passed, the government came up with new and more complicated ways to crack down on fraudulent physicians and create healthcare reform, making it harder for the doctor to get paid, by making him/her prove every single thing they did was legitimate. By creating a book of procedures, they gave us 100,000 five- digit codes to learn, that had to be appended to a claim form to tell the insurance company in computer lingo that an office visit and or

43

procedure happened. Then a diagnosis had to be selected out of thousands and it had to be specific and support the office visit or it was considered non-payable. To make things even more monotonous, the worker had to call the insurance companies and ask for permission, mind you, for the very patients the doctors wanted to treat. It's now called prior-authorization and it is not a guarantee for payment.

During your exams your doctor talks to you about your present illness, right? Where does it hurt, how long, timing, location, is it chronic or not chronic, modifying factors (did you do something to modify the condition), then they move into your review of systems. Check here if you ever had diabetes, high blood pressure, musculoskeletal pain, do you have difficulty urinating, do you have HIV? Do you sneeze a lot, bleed from the vagina or rectum, experience stomach pain, feel breast pain, lumps bumps bruises? Then from there, they ask about your past medical history, your social history (do you drink or smoke), and your past family history.

Then you finally get the examination. Did they check your throat that was sore, look in your eyes, your ears, tap your reflexes, take your blood pressure, height, weight, and calculate your BMI?

Listen to your heart? Sorry, but you're still not done. Now the doctor must ponder and graph all of this information into our computer world to justify how high of a code they can charge for your particular case. So now he/she has to determine how many diagnoses they assigned you, if it was your first time in 3 years (new patient). Then complexity of medical data he/she had to review such as x-rays, other doctors' records, test results, and if there was a plan for a surgical procedure. It doesn't hurt to say how much time they spent with you in the room, either. Many of us have seen them say they did all of the above, yet they were in and out of the room in 5 minutes which defies logic.

All of these things add up to how much they are going to charge you. The patient example I mentioned above is a 99204 (new patient detailed level) She was given a script for stomach pain with an appointment to follow-up with a cat scan in 2 weeks if not better. If not better, then surgery would be eminent and that would be a code 47562 which is worth more, and don't forget the diagnosis code. If I told you how every number means something, you would rather watch paint dry. Maybe you'll have a new appreciation for medical staff when you see the hoops they must jump through to capture the doctor's documentation and have it mean something to the insurance carriers so that they will pay your bill. It didn't take long before I was leaving Ruth sticky notes because she did not want to learn all of these new rules. She quit when I began leaving instructions on the computer; for her it was tortuous.

Since we're so computerized now, we can take all that writing of what we did and make it into something legible, give the insurance companies the codes they want, both diagnostic and evaluation and management, at which point it is supposed to miraculously morph into a check a few weeks down the line as long as you play the rules and file the claims in electronic format that is HIPAA compliant. (HIPAA protects your privacy). Surely this diatribe made you yawn. I know I am thinking about bed, finally. Hang tight, because the sticky note office had some outrageous moments. Next time you pick up this book, you will meet Arnie and Cindy; two of the most entertaining people I have met to date.

Chapter 8 Arnie and Cindy

I promised you Arnie and Cindy. I'll leave their last names anonymous, but they were a big part of my first clinical experience behind the desk. Arnie and Cindy were lovers since Junior-High School; (middle school.) Arnie had a twin brother named Joel but that's where the similarities ended. While Joel inherited the slender, athletic body, Arnie inherited the brain, but without common sense. Some of the sharpest people I know had a disproportionate amount of their skills go to the intellectual side, but little on the reasoning side.

Arnie had a club foot and as a result, had to wear a thick soled club foot shoe. Given that his left leg was so much shorter, it could be awkward at times. (I felt bad for his disability but knew he would not appreciate pity.) Since he was not of an athletic build like Joel, most of his weight was distributed his hips. He literally was shaped like a pear.

Cindy was a wonderful wife to him, calling him morning and night from her office at a college where she was a psychologist. Cindy was a slender woman, who reminded me of a flower child from the 60's. She had a very high pitched voice with an East coast accent. She wore Birkenstock sandals and had kind of messy long hair, and wore flowing floral skirts and breezy blouses.

When Cindy would call the office to speak to Arnie, we would know it was her by the way his voice rolled up into a little boy pitch and he lovingly chirped "Hi-iiiiiii Ciiiiinnnnndeeeeeee. Oh I love you too, oh no you don't. I do; nope this much." About this time, I would fake a gag with my hands around my throat, sending my co-worker into a laughing conniption.

What a lovely pair, really. It was heartwarming to see two professional people dote on each other the way they did. Did I happen to mention they did not waste anything? If they could squeeze a penny, they would. Maybe because of all the insurance rules I mentioned in the previous chapter; who knows?

If you are wondering why I am rambling on about stochastic topics, it's because feeding you this dribble may sufficiently distract you from whatever is jetting through your mind and keeping you wakeful. Well maybe I shouldn't have reminded you about that; bring your mind back to Arnie and Cindy!

Arnie and Cindy stories are entertaining, yet dull. (No need to thank me, just go to sleep!)

As I mentioned, Arnie and Cindy did not spend money unnecessarily. To their credit, they lived mid-town and not in the foothills, took vacations only in the summer, and drove old Toyota cars and a Minnie Winnie RV for family vacations.

The medical office was a house he bought: another asset. The entryway had a little half wall which looked directly into the dining room, which was used as the reception/office worker area. The living room, complete with stacked rock fireplace was the waiting room. The 3 bedrooms down the hall to the right were the examination rooms. Behind the reception area was the kitchen, and to the opposite side of the bedrooms was an enclosed double carport which Arnie used for his office, and I suspect his liaisons with Cindy.

The hallway leading from the kitchen to the bedrooms had a series of built-in cabinets lining the right side, which we used for medical supplies. The cabinets had 4" vertical handles on them. This was a 70's house all the way, complete with multi-colored shag carpet, lime green walls in one bedroom, orange in another, and the requisite dark paneling in Arnie's office. Renovation was not in the foreseeable future.

Our note pads were scratch paper cut into squares, stacked up, which Arnie would then glue to make like notebooks. We never bought scratch paper the 7 years I was in his employ. And, I never wrote on an 8 x 11 piece of paper: our scratch paper was 4" x 6", precisely. Our luxury was the sticky notes: Ruth, his faithful employee continued to paper the desk with them for me throughout her tenure. I felt like she was Captain Kangaroo reincarnated. For those of you who don't know who Captain Kangaroo was; he was a children's television celebrity who had notes pinned on his jacket which he would pull off to tell kids what was up next.

When I had a baby, Arnie and Cindy visited me with a bunch of dusty royal blue plastic flowers and Fannie Farmer candies that were so old they were like rocks: the inside of the box was covered in mold. He presented these to me as if they were precious jewels. He was so proud. I later learned from my co-worker that he had found them in the shed at the office. He ran his hand over the box of chocolates like a model on the Price is Right. He and Cindy were generally proud of their felicitous gift.

Sometimes the colleges would call and say they had a cadaver and where did he want the arms sawn off? I'd trudge into his office to ask for his response. He'd contemplate while slowly lifting his round butt cheek up from the chair, rip a silent but deadly to burn my eyes, and then say," have them cut them off at the shoulders and bend them at the elbows." Arnie would stare intently at me as if daring me to mention the dreaded fart. What had I gone in there to ask him? I had lost my focus so distracted I was by the red heat traveling up my neck.

Later in the week, the arms would arrive wrapped in gauze and red plastic bags. Arnie would toss the arms into our employee fridge, which was a little camp fridge. There was no way to put your food in there and not have the arms embrace it. (Can anyone say personal cooler?)

Arnie would bring in his granola bars and muffins and toss them in on the arms. Since the arms were lonely, creepy, and next to the copy machine, I would talk to them when I was there alone. I decided it would be appropriate to name them Freddie. So the games began, "Freddie have you hugged your child today? Freddie reach out and touch someone.

Freddie, you need a manicure". Humor kept the circumstances manageable.

One day the Doctor picked up a dozen homemade blueberry muffins from Costco and tossed them in the fridge on top of Freddie. Gross Gross Gross!!!! Over the ensuing weeks the muffins became pungent and moldy. Common sense told me to throw them out. This served to get me a tongue lashing. I was not to waste that food. Arnie marched over to the fridge, grabbed a muffin, pulled his scalpel out of his lab coat pocket and held it while he heated the muffin up in the microwave. The office became permeated with a perfumey smell. Arnie took his muffin to his desk and proceeded to dissect the mold with his scalpel by using a flicking method. He ate the rest. Again, hands around throat and gag while my co-worker and I doubled over.

Arnie and Cindy did so many things that to write enough to bore you could be a book in itself. One of the best was when he created a sexual board game for their anniversary but forgot he left all the game pieces he was copying in the copy machine. (At least I hope he forgot it was there: that is a repugnant thought)! Imagine my surprise as I innocently opened the copier and found a game board in there saying "move 3 spaces to the right and remove your shirt, move 2 spaces to the left and favor me with this". Can you hear my scream? (No one was there but Freddie). I rapidly loaded the pieces back into the copier, waited for the doctor to arrive, and confidentially mentioned that he had something in the copier he may wish to remove. He seemed to enjoy my discomfiture, kind of like the noxious farts.

I have one more item to tell you about in my office life with Arnie. He insisted on taking his patients back to the examination rooms himself. The cast room was bedroom #1: royal blue. The post-operative room was lime green, bedroom #2. Bedroom #3 was orange: our other storage area.

Arnie's pet peeve was when a patient was late. He would stomp out of his office, up to my desk and demand to know where said patient was. On one particular morning a patient checked in with me and then went into the restroom which was across the hall from Arnie's cast room and attached to the end of the waiting area. Arnie was not pleased to see that his patient was not sitting meekly in the waiting room for her visit when he came out for her. I explained that she was in the rest room. Rolling his eyes and sighing, he grabbed her chart, opened it, and planted himself outside the bathroom door. She nearly collided with him when she walked out. I was extremely embarrassed for that poor patient.

There's so much to regale you with about Arnie and Cindy that we'll break this into two chapters. We will have to do our next chapter on our entertaining pair.

Chapter 9-More Arnie

Both Arnie and Cindy were artistic. For a chandelier, the waiting room had a huge Styrofoam cupped fixture hanging long and low on a gold chain, over a side table. It probably measured at least 2 feet from the radius. The Styrofoam cups were glued together into a spherical shape with alternating blue and green sheer fabric pasted over the open ends of each cup. When patients would comment on the lamp, Arnie would glow brighter than the muted cups, confident they were giving him accolades for a wonderful piece of art.

Also in that room hanging over the fireplace was a pair of hands, palms up, together, holding a ball of fire. When visiting professionals would look at the picture, Arnie would pick it up and say "can you feel the heat' it exudes warmth; this should be in every hand therapy office; very therapeutic, yes very therapeutic." Each visitor replied appropriately and occasionally some of them genuinely seemed drawn in.

Now that you have this setting in mind, you're probably asking yourself, *how in the world did you manage to work there for 7 years?* My answer is simple: Sheer entertainment! I had a co-worker to share the mirth with and we never ceased to laugh until we cried. Arnie and Cindy created a diversion from a ho-hum occupation. Note; this was not the sticky note co-worker who had left our employ. I always wondered why Arnie paid for all those sticky notes.

My co-worker, Anna, and I would make wagers about Cindy. Would she appear today? Would she be in her leather sandals, would she color her hair, would she manage to drag our fingernails down the chalkboard with her high shrill voice? For the record, Cindy never failed to disappoint. She would march into the office; treat us like we were their servants, breeze into Arnie's office, where the door would close and the high little girl giggles would begin. You guessed it: we were making the retching motions.

One day Anna and I wagered that Arnie would appear to work in the same clothes the next day. He generally wore brown worn pleated front slacks, and a wrinkled button up the front shirt. He did not let us down. Tuesday came and Arnie was still wearing the tired slacks and shirt. The brown pants continued to appear for the next 3 weeks until the day of the dreaded catch.

Arnie was in a hurry to get to an examination room. As I mentioned, he has a club foot, so his gait is not of the most graceful variety. As he swung to the left to sweep into the examination room, his pants caught the handle on the hallway cabinet to his right. Anna and I heard a loud mutter and footsteps coming back toward our office. Arnie had a 4" x 6" rip on the seat of his pants (just like our scratch pads), and asked Anna to tape his butt. I am not kidding: she had to scotch tape the gaping tear, at which point he proceeded to see patients the remainder of the day. At no time did he put on his medical coat to cover up the rent and tape. He honestly had no clue at how ridiculous he looked.

Don't think too hard about what I'm going to tell you next, but I'm wondering if you can guess what our next wager was about to be? You got it: whether or not he was going to replace those pants. Anna bet that he would take them to a tailor and I told her that was ludicrous. It was not on a seam, the fabric was threadbare as it was, and they had their day in the sun.

The next morning, Arnie came into the office with a different pair of pants on, although still wrinkled. I do not think he nor did Cindy believed in irons as they were a waste of time. Vain, they were not.

Do you know what he was holding? A bag! And inside were the brown pants. I know what his request was? It was to take those pants to the tailor and see if they could match the thread and mend the slacks. I did NOT want to go to a tailor and verbalize such a petition! Even the tailor couldn't want the business that bad. Anna and I played paper rock scissors and I won. And yes, the tailor repaired them and Arnie was thrilled the thread matched exactly! It must have been an old spool they found in a warehouse if it could match that faded brown. I'm sure he and Cindy were pleased, as it was money saved that they could use elsewhere. You'd think they were a one-income family on a limited budget, but such was not the case.

Previously I mentioned that Cindy was a Psychologist. She was employed at a Junior College and dealt with all manner of the human psyche phenomenon. Cindy was trained to help people cope with stress and give them the tools to react suitably.

One day the phone rang and Cindy was hysterically screaming on the other end of the line. There had been an incident on the news that upset her. Cindy's emotions were out of control. She was screaming so high and loudly into the phone, I thought she was dying. Her screaming continued, so I put her on hold and got Arnie on the line. I could hear the decibels in Arnie's voice rise in tandem with Cindy's. They were both inconsolable.

After the call, Cindy somehow managed to get to the office. By then she was chanting over and over, it's terrible, it's terrible, it's terrible in reference to the news story. She had no coping skills, whatsoever. All I could think about was how in the world was she to help her students when she reacted in a like that? When is it appropriate to act out, versus being reasonable, calm, and level-headed?

Arnie came to the rescue. Once off the phone, he used his craft as a Shuman priest to begin a meditative chant. As a sobbing Cindy flew into his arms, I heard the chant, "Om, Shanti Shanti Shanti Om". Soon, all was well in the Arnie-Cindy world once again and for once, Anna and I were rendered speechless. I won't bore you with their summers in

Bali living with the Shaman priest in a tent, the rituals, and $5 massages.

Are you bored or entertained? Maybe we need a topic in our next chapter that is a bit drier.

Chapter 10: Hunting and Scouting for Animals

There may be masses of you who lay in bed and wonder how do you scout for an animal? This chapter will give you some ideas.

How do we go from Arnie and Cindy to animals? It defies logic, but that's just how the human mind functions. Mine jumps from topic to topic in a typical disorderly fashion. It was not hard to make the leap. Cindy was out of control, she was howling with angst, and Arnie managed to soothe her with a chant. It reminded me of a horse whisperer, calming the savage beast. And what is a beast, but an animal? A beast implies a wild animal, as does howling. To me, it was a logical ratiocination. Yes, I know, what is ratiocination? If I don't answer that question, you will be ruminating about that and not following the topic of scouting for animals.

Ratiocination is a systematic and methodical way of reasoning.

What would you consider to be a beast? Is it always of the animal variety? Is it something large, such as an enormous dog? Could it be a manner of behavior that is uncivilized? How about domesticated versus wild?

When dealing with wild animals, there are various reasons one might want to scout for an animal. Perhaps it's to hunt for food, tag for research, simply to observe in their environment, or maybe a heroic act to save others from an animal that has previously attacked humans.

Scouting is a method that allows one to gather information about their prey. (Is this too interesting? Maybe I should use larger words, not give their definitions, and lose you in the details?)

As you prepare for your reconnoitering, you will need a list of items to aid you in your reconnaissance mission. The questions to establish are: what you are surveying, why, how dangerous is your beast, what is the climate going to be, the terrain, and how long do you give yourself to be out in the field?

For purposes of discussion, let's say you are seeking a rabid coyote that attacked not only domestic chickens, but also an adult male. The coyote was last seen in the foothills of a mountainous community, about 5000 feet in elevation. It is the acme of summer in a humid climate.

What provisions do you think would be needed for this expedition? Perhaps you should know more about your subject? Are coyotes nocturnal or diurnal? What would you use to attract a coyote?

Coyotes are typically nocturnal, although they can be baited during the late afternoon or early morning. From my experience, coyotes will eat almost anything. I've heard they like dog food as well as watermelon. For this exercise, coyotes are probably the easiest to scout. You wouldn't need many supplies at all to track one, because you can pretty much get them to come to you. However, in our scenario, the coyote is not in a residential area, but in a mountainous area where the houses are on several acres or more, thus allowing it to assault domestic chickens, goats, and other animals, as well as the person on the hiking trail.

The best way to scout this animal is to put out pretty much any type of food just before nightfall so the coyote beats the hawks, possums and raccoons to the bait. Be prepared to patiently wait, out of sight and downwind so they do not smell you instead of your lure.

Coyotes travel in packs and from what I've observed spread out after they have seen their live prey to prepare their trap. In this case, I would think a rabid coyote is more likely to travel alone.

If you are not into shooting live animals, wild or otherwise, then use a collarum to humanely trap the animal. Collarums are specifically meant for the canine species. Since coyote habits are fairly easy to ascertain, it would not be necessary to go observe them first, then return when you understand.

This scouting mission would be as simple as setting your bait right outside your collarum and waiting. Before the night is half over, your rabid coyote should be trapped. Personally, I'd shoot the coyote, since a rabid coyote is not one I would want to rehabilitate. If this upsets your sensibilities, then go with me on the collarum idea.

If you are a hunter and do not track your prey, such as an elk or a deer, it could be one long hunting session. Perhaps that is your goal: stay out longer and go home and say "I'm sorry honey, but they were onto us: it took so much longer to track than we had anticipated". .

Tracking can be a lot of fun in and of itself for those of you who do not desire to shoot a wild animal with anything more than a camera. It requires a lot of patience, the ability to walk or climb long distances,

64

as well as the temperament to remain still for extended periods of time to get that perfect shot.

If you plan on being gone more than a day then perhaps a 4 wheel drive quad to rent and hold your supplies would be a good idea, although they create noise and you would still need to stage the quads at an agreed upon location. Do not travel alone, and make sure you know where your partner is at all times... Dick Cheney anyone?

Have food provisions, shelter, ammunition, binoculars, sufficient camera battery life, and clothing for the number of days you set aside. Be prepared to go home with or without your objective reached and enjoy the sheer adventure of the wilderness. Set yourself realistic goals. Day 1 you will remain at the camp site and simply be the sentry. Day 2 you could act upon your day 1 results, and on.

If you are a hunter, be prepared to have a way to transport your meat back to your vehicle. Are you planning on having a taxidermist mount the head? Are you going to skin the carcass at the campsite or do this at an appointed place? How much time do you have to skin the animal? Do you leave it there, mark it with something that smells like you to discourage bears, and return to retrieve it? If it's an area with bear, for example, should you have parachute rope or another apparatus to string it at least 100 feet away from the carcass and off the ground?

For you photographers, which would be me, did you get a wide angle lens, zoom, and take the picture in as many frames as possible? Do you have enough shots to take this back to your dark room or developer to ensure you do not need another night out to get the correct lighting and view?

So when scouting, remember to be pragmatic, understand your objective, and be patient. Return home with the attitude that you accomplished your goal. Do not be discouraged that you are back to your daily grind if you prefer to be out in the wild. Plan your next trip and give yourself something to anticipate as you lay in bed wishing you were not still awake. It makes the insomnia tolerable. Go home, and if you are married, think of ways you can make life easier for your spouse so that when it's time to go scouting again, they will not mind.

One of the best tasks you can do is chores. Ever hear of the book "Sex Begins in the Kitchen" by Dr. Kevin Leman? Maybe you could do a better job loading and emptying the dishwasher. Chapter 11 will give you tips on how to win those brownie points.

Chapter 11: Brownie points: The Art of Loading a Dishwasher and more

My husband likes to load and unload the dishwasher. This act gains positive marks with me. I hate to unload the dishwasher, but when I do, I like it to be organized to make the job much less tiresome.

Although my husband assists with the dishwasher, he also annoys me by washing every single dish with the water running in the sink, making them appear clean; I can't tell if the dishwasher has been run by opening it and taking a peek inside. To be greener, I tell him, maybe we could just dip them in a sink of water to rinse off and not run the water: kind of like when you brush your teeth. It's a habit I can't break him of and since I don't want to be his mother I suck it up. To cope, we put a magnet on the refrigerator. If it's on the front of the refrigerator right side up, the dishes are clean. We liked the idea of putting a magnet on the front of the dishwasher, but the front is not magnetic, so no dice there. If you have an investigative mind, this little tidbit let you know we do not have stainless steel appliances. Some magnets are literally pictures of a dishwasher that have "clean" on one end and "dirty" on the other, thus making the flipping unmistakable. I use a magnet my daughter gave me, because I refuse to give it up so I assigned the magnet a purpose.

I am wandering from our topic, once again, so back to the loading. There truly is a correct way to load a dishwasher. Face the dishes toward the center so that the spray hits the soiled spots, directly. Do not imitate the commercials where you have a contest with your teenage child to see if you can squeeze in just one more plate and there will be nothing to hand wash. The tighter your dishes are crammed into the dishwasher, the harder it is for the spray to hit the full surface area.

Some dishwashers have built in garbage disposers, while others are connected to the sink disposal. The sink disposal is not a substitute for not rinsing your dishes. It is there for the final rinse to flush out the sink, but its function is not to be a disposal. The dishwashers without a disposal could get chunks of food past the dishwasher filter and into the spray or pump and clog it up. If you do have a dishwasher with a built in disposal it will chew up the debris on the dishes, which will assist the loader into not prewashing and rinsing the dishes prior to filling up the appliance.

You could really milk this with your significant other and tell them how you carefully cleaned the filter in the dishwasher, pre-rinsed the dishes, and saved significant money by not having to purchase an expensive appliance with all the bells and whistles. Whether or not they'll buy this story, is another discussion altogether. I value my husband's time with me more than the extra time he labors over the dishwasher.

I most appreciate the proper loading of dishes by category, because when I have to unload the dishwasher, I want to grab all the cups and knock out that cupboard, then all the plates, all the large utensils and this is the best one: we rock at how we load silverware. Your dishwasher should give you plenty of compartments to separate your silverware by type. Load your silverware handle down, with the exception of knives. With the tines of your fork sticking straight up, they capture the spray. Knives are pointed down for safety. I have been told that dishwashers can dull your knives, so I typically hand wash mine. When the silverware is sorted by type, I grab the handful of forks and plop them into the corresponding slot in the utensil drawer, same with the teaspoons, soup spoons, butter knives, and utensils. I happen to hate butter, actually, so there aren't any butter knives; it saves me a slot! Unloading is a piece of cake. I don't exactly come unhinged when I unload other people's dishwashers and the silverware is all mixed together, but it certainly bugs me about the extra time it takes.

The type of dishwasher detergent used also makes a difference on the cleanliness of your dishes. Certain types of detergent do not dissolve as readily. If you're mid-cycle, take a peek and see if the detergent is breaking down or if it's still in its original state. (Do you ever open the dishwasher mid-cycle just to get a nice steam sauna for your skin? I stick my head in there, take a deep breath, and stay that way until my face feels moisturized and then I forget I was in there to check the detergent.) I use a gel product. Some prefer the tablets because they contain other additives enhancing the sparkle of your dishes. Since I like to save money, I use white vinegar in the compartment where you would normally add the spot free rinse agent. It all depends on how hard your water is. I use white vinegar for everything! Kind of like the father in "My Big Fat Greek Wedding" and his passion for all things Windex.

While we're on the topic of water, it should be hot. The hotter the cleaner, my dad always said. When we hand- washed dishes as kids, it would be rubber glove time because we were required to wash the dishes at the hottest possible temperature in order to sterilize them. I still buy off on that and throw my toothbrush in the dishwasher. Sometimes I feel guilty because if I was eating off the plates at someone else's house and knew that they had been washed with their germy toothbrush, it would bother me. That's pretty much an irrational thought, as the forks and spoons were also in people's mouths. I don't have my dog eat off the dishes and then serve them to people, or vomit in the sauce pan and then pop it in the dishwasher. (I know people who do this, but it's not me people; it's not me!) Speaking of germs, what about other ways to assist and make your brownie points?

If you are the one in the household who does not clean toilets, then listen up. From my experience, it's the women who clean the toilets. Men what is up with this? Do you not give that bowl equal time? Why is it not your responsibility to assist in tidying that particular spot of the house? It warms the cockles of my heart when I see a gleaming shining sparkly toilet bowl. Unfortunately, I can only give the accolades to myself as my husband has abhorrence to all things resembling toilet brushes. Being a germ-phobe is not an excuse, since there are products out there where you can push a button on a long wand and dispense of the disposable cleaning head right down the toilet. Clean the toilet bowl, the seat, and under the seat and your partner will be stunned.

Now that the dishwasher is loaded, run through its cycle, emptied and the toilets are clean, what else would be a real boost for brownie points? (This is a rhetorical question: do not think hard about an answer or it will defeat the purpose of my babble.) There are a couple of immediate ones I can think of and do not think they are gender specific: I love it when my husband gives me a massage. It allows me to relax and unwind after a tough day. It means he appreciates that I, too, need TLC.

How about a light back massage that does not turn into foreplay (men), and doesn't make them yelp when you hit their pressure points (women). Complete the massage, make it the way they like it, and then see where the results take you. I'm not talking about every single day, but once in a while to change things up and maybe even help them sleep. Perhaps they will be grateful.

The word grateful should make you contemplative right now. Think about that with a smile on your face and consider the possibilities. I'm trying so hard right now not to add a smiley face to this text, but even I am not that cheesy! Speaking of cheese, makes me think about cooking and cooking makes me think of so many funny stories to plant in your mind and distract you. I could literally do stand-up comedy about the many situations my husband puts himself into.

Chapter 12: My husband: Fodder

Do you have someone in your life that just hands you the straight lines and simply does not have a clue when it comes to certain tasks? In our household, it's my husband. He is not handy at all and is absolutely lost if he must find his way around any domesticated chore without step by step guidance. This includes anything inside or outside the house, and most definitely in the kitchen.

He is so easily confused and his downfall is that he won't ask for direction, because that's not macho. And the result is that he tries to puzzle it out by himself.

There are so many stories to regale you with, but I will limit it to a few. Although these stories are not tedious, they may be sufficient to derail your current thought process.

You probably know someone who is without culinary skills and you wonder how in the world they survive(d) on their own. Let me introduce Ron to you.

When I met Ron he was active duty military. He relied on fast food or the chow hall on base for his sustenance. I learned to cook as a young child, so it is second nature to me. Additionally, when I was growing up, girls were required to take cooking and sewing class while the boys took shop and woodworking. Nevertheless, the "boy" skills did not stick with Ron, either. To his credit, once he is shown how to perform a task, he will be able to successfully complete it, but it will be slow and laborious.

My favorite saying about Ron's culinary skills is that he can't cook, but he can stir. I'm serious. No matter what I'm cooking on the stove, Ron will feel the desire to assist me. He will pick up a spoon or spatula, (no, not my mom's spatula), and begin stirring whatever it is that is on the stove. He will stir without pausing, prompting a gentle reminder to take some time between stirring these entrees so that the heat can reach the food.

We have found some positives out of these excursions into the kitchen, such as making tacos. As I was browning the hamburger one time, Ron picked up the spatula and vigorously began chopping at the meat, breaking it into a consistency representing a fast food taco shop. What I noticed was that the meat actually was quite good so finely chopped, and that I lacked the patience to hover over the skillet to stir and chop as Ron did. I added the spices, and he continued to stir. We found a success. Ron will forevermore be the taco meat stirrer. When I'm frying potatoes, he flips them so often; they do not brown, so he is off potato duty. You get the idea.

I happen to love iced tea so Ron bought me an iced tea maker thinking that would aid me in my penchant for that particular kind of beverage. He saw me make it many times. If you have not used an iced tea maker, you may not fully appreciate what I am about to tell you, but in a nutshell, you use it much as you would a coffee maker.

One day, Ron thought he would surprise me when I got home from work and have a fresh glass of iced tea waiting for me. Once I got in the door, he seemed perplexed and frustrated. When I inquired as to why, he mentioned that the iced tea maker he bought me was no longer working. I proceeded to investigate said tea maker myself and discovered that indeed, it had produced clear water: no sign of tea at all in the pitcher. I did what I thought anyone would do; I lifted the lid of the machine to take a peek into the filter area housing the teabags to see if it was plugged up somehow. To my delight, the tea was indeed in the filter; however, Ron had not opened the paper covering the Lipton teabags, so the water was simply flowing around the still sealed teabags. Much to his chagrin, I bent over in giggles (not good for the male ego, by the way), and choked out that you had to remove the teabag from its wrapping, first.

There must be something about wrappings that throws my husband off. On yet another occasion I asked him if he could get the rice started while I was held over at the office. I felt quite confident with this request as it was the easiest rice on the market to make. It's called "Success" and in our case, that was an oxymoron. My first mistake was to assume the outcome would be successful.

Many of you have seen the boil in the bag rice and know the process has been greatly simplified for the busy cook. I would buy Success rice. The rice is sealed in a perforated bag with a little tab on the end for pulling it out of the water. This is the product he was using. The following are verbatim stovetop instructions from the box.

"1. Pour about 1 quart of water into medium saucepan and submerge 1 bag of rice. Bring water to a boil and boil uncovered 8-10 minutes.

2. Remove bag from water with fork and drain. Cut open bag and empty rice into serving dish."

This time I received a text from Ron: "call home when you get a chance." I dialed him right away, having no idea what I would hear. Ron was discouraged because the rice wasn't thickening and it was really watery. I could not imagine how in the world boil in a bag rice could be watery. I ran through the process in my mind and began to fire questions at him. "Did you use a medium saucepan and fill it about 2/3 with water?" He replied to the affirmative. Next question: "How long did you boil it for?" He said, "8-10 minutes". One more question. "Did you wait for the water to boil, first?" Another affirmative. Now I'm perplexed. I decided to try a different tactic and asked Ron to explain to me what he did. All was well until he said he opened the bag of rice and poured it in the water.

I was faced with a dilemma. Do I peel into giggles again and hurt his feelings, or do I take a big breath and explain why emptying pre-measured rice in a bag into a pan full of water may not work. I ended up doing both.

What is the moral to this story? Do not make your subject feel ridiculed or they will not attempt rice again. In fact, in an effort for peace and democracy, Ron has offered to stay out of the cooking realm, and in exchange will wash the dishes. That's a fair compromise, right? Did you not read chapter 11?

Here's one of my favorites. Ron and I both enjoy a nice fresh plump cantaloupe. Typically I will halve it, remove the seeds, and then cut each half into fourths, using a knife to remove the fleshy melon slices.

I had some work to do and Ron wanted to relieve some of my stress. He asked if there was something he could do to help. I jumped at the offer and asked him if he could prep a cantaloupe for our dinner. He gave me a big smile and said he'd be happy to do that.

Thirty minutes later my errand was completed. I found Ron in the kitchen still working on the cantaloupe; the counter was covered in juice, seeds and pieces of rind. It was a huge mess! I absorbed the cantaloupe massacre in front of me and noticed that he had been peeling the melon like an orange. I had no words and still don't. I felt my heart go out to him.

Ron's latest challenge is to learn to cook because our brother-n-law who cooks very well innocently remarked in response to our praise of his culinary skills that "anyone who can read can cook." The gauntlet has been thrown and I just know there are more stories in our future, because in order to read you must know what the words, blend, mix, chop, dice, pare, and slice mean. He tried the *slicing* part and because he used a forceful downward motion, the item was crushed.

My husband being the standup guy he is, he feels the need to contribute more than doing dishes and stirring. I happen to detest dusting and since he doesn't, win-win, right? (I have a feeling you're catching on). No, not right. The first time Ron dusted our house, he used an entire can of furniture polish. Not only was the wood gleaming, shiny, and thick with wax, you could skate on the tile floors around the furniture. And it took him about 90 minutes. In that amount of time, I can get the whole house clean!

Bored To Sleep

I determined that next time Ron dusted, I would observe more closely. I stealthily watched the procedure; I noticed he sprayed all up and down the outside of every piece of furniture, even if it was a leg. The sides of our furniture were never so clean. He went over pictures, tops of entertainment centers I never could reach, and even the television sets (and yes, I'm aware you don't use furniture polish on television sets, but they were dust free!) I was impressed, yet horrified at what a huge chore it had become for him. Eventually he caught on and although it takes him an inordinately long time to dust, we still have polish left in the can at the end of each session.

Bear in mind: Ron is a gentleman. If we go to a store, he insists on carrying the heaviest packages. If I grab the bags while he is putting the receipt and card back in his wallet, he'll hurriedly put his hands out and take more than half the bags from me. He thinks it is a travesty to have his wife carrying the load while he does nothing. I love him for that and with this context of his character; I understand that he needs to help. It's in his DNA.

When I mop, I can get it done in no time: it's merely years of experience. Ron feels he should vacuum AND dust so that I only have to mop; (and clean toilets!) Yes it means I have to wait for him to get that done first, which means I have to find something else to do while I wait. The hurry is now over. I remember how important this is to Ron, so I back off.

Oh my! This is Ron's method. Turn on the vacuum cleaner and start in a room at one end of the house. The furniture polish is at hand and once he gets to the end of about two rows in a room, he turns off the vacuum cleaner to turn it around and then heads down the next path. In the midst of this switching the machine off and on, he stops and dusts whatever he moves beside. His method can literally take him most of the morning, because a few of the rooms have television sets in them. To make it more interesting, the televisions are flipped onto his favorite sports station and he captures the highlights as he switches the vacuum off to dust which I suspect is his whole motivation.

Ever an optimist, I thought maybe painting would be a great task for Ron. It's methodical, and doesn't require artistic flair if the color and walls have been pre-determined. And, I must say, he can paint well: just very slowly. I can have 3 walls done to his one wall and that's being generous. Our compromise here is that I trim in and he rolls: believe it or not this works.

Speaking of trimming, one day when I was at work and Ron was at home, he decided to trim back an oleander bush (the size of a tree) that was encroaching upon the diving board end of the pool. When I came home and looked out the window, I realized something was amiss. The beautiful lush flowered tree had been given a crew cut. It was pared down to its main trunk: all the leaves and branches were missing. Thinking maybe this was just because Ron loves diving and didn't want it near the board, I didn't think too much of it the until the next time he offered to trim some bushes. But alas! The bushes disappeared, too. The big joke in our house now is to keep the pruning shears away from him or the poor plant will not survive. And never ask for a haircut!

I would be negligent if I didn't share our lawn mowing experience with you. We lived in Arizona during our early years of marriage. We raked rocks and sprayed weeds: we did not have grass. However, I was born and raised a Midwest girl, and Ron was from California. Both of us had grass to mow when we were kids, but the difference was that Ron wasn't required to cut grass as I was. A few years into our marriage Ron was given a 3 year assignment of duty in England with the Air Force. A whole new world of duties: primarily cutting the grass.

The British homes we lived in didn't have huge yards, but as a military member there were standards to be upheld such as a neat yard, with the borders edged. We decided an electric lawnmower would be just fine for these purposes along with a weed eater. I cut the grass in rows, always keeping the cord behind me as I turned to make the next pass. . The job was fast and easy: all cut in a precise grid-like pattern.

The first time Ron offered to cut the grass I explained how I did it and that it would take about 15-20 minutes. I am not kidding! 90 minutes later I finally caved and went outside, having successfully ignored the sounds I was hearing outside. There was a pattern cut in the grass that could easily rival the alien crop circles in the UK. This is not an exaggeration; the neat rows were absent. Evidently, that darn cord kept tripping him up. At the end of each pass, he would turn off the lawnmower, move the cord around and then start in a new area. Off and on, off and on; just like the vacuum cleaner.

Bored To Sleep

We have been married another 10 years since England and just today we had two more Ron incidents. Our leaves were out of control on the front lawn. We drove around the neighborhood and only our home had two old trees dumping leaves prematurely. There are elderly ladies in a few of the homes across from us and as the wind blows the leaves across the street toward their pristine yards, I see them going outside, daily, to stoop over, pick them up or reach for a rake much too large for them as they look toward the source of the leaves. We're new to the neighborhood and I honestly don't want to be on their bad sides: these ladies pull no punches!

I talked Ron into mowing the leaves rather than raking, by attaching our leaf bag which we previously had only used for grass clippings. We discussed that he'd have to check it often because it would probably fill up quickly and lose its effectiveness. After I could tell he had cut several rows I went out to check the bag and saw there was still a little room in it. I know I should have just left him alone, but anytime it's a new endeavor, Ron doesn't always compute until he's seen the results. Anyway, I left him to it, went back to my trimming while he continued to go and for once he hadn't shut the mower off. When I went to see what was going on, bits of leaves were spraying out the bottom of the mower but he was unaware. We took the bag off and leaves were overflowing everywhere. Yes, it was not effective; he had a trail behind him. So I did what any inquiring mind would do; I asked him why he hadn't emptied it. His response was "because I thought it would tell me." (No answer there).

All that yard work made us hungry so we decided to grill burgers on our new charcoal grill. I left Ron to it because he does a decent job with a gas barbecue, so I wasn't worried. Since it was just the two of us, we were only going to have burgers for us. Ron was supposed to start the charcoal and then come into the house to assist me with all the sides but he never came in. When I went to check on him and saw flames were shooting up at least 4 feet from the top of the grill endangering everything around it. The heat was immense. He was just standing there with his hands in his pockets watching it. I said, "I wondered where you were; why are you watching those flames go out of control?" He said, "Well as long as I watch it they should be fine." I replied, "But you shouldn't have to stand there and watch it; why are the flames so high; how much charcoal did you use?" Ron had dumped an entire medium sized bag into a medium sized grill, doused the pre-lit briquettes with charcoal lighter and then proceeded to wait for the flames to go down, but those flames were going nowhere: they were well fed not to mention overkill for burgers for two. Once we got the lid on the grill down using some rather creative ways to get close enough, the flames were literally licking out from under the lid, the sides, anywhere they could escape.

Today was a day of demonstrations. Ron is an enormously intelligent man, so I know that down the road I will never have to write about leaf bags and charcoal again. He is visual and he got it. For me, these instances make it hard to not be controlling, but I'm trying to have a sense of humor: it's kind of cute!

I have one or two last Ron stories to bore you with. I have to stop or my husband will be humiliated beyond all belief. Thank goodness he has a great sense of humor.

The other day I had started doing laundry but didn't quite finish by the end of the day. I had already pre-sorted the clothes that had been in our single hamper. I explained to Ron that the clothes basket I used to carry the clothes up and down the stairs had the whites in it and the hamper had the darks. If he didn't mind, could he put his clothes in the appropriate bin tonight? (I have never made this request before or since we only have the one hamper.) I would finish the laundry in the morning.

I finished the laundry the next day. Two days later, I realized he was still sorting his clothes: whites in the basket that still happened to be in our room and darks in the hamper, even though I myself was tossing everything into the hamper. I think he thought this was forevermore: he didn't question; he just did it. Now I suspect nothing will even make it to the hamper because he is that confused. Ron is a literal man and by now I should understand that.

Our bed has a duvet comforter on the top: the type that barely extends over the sides and isn't meant to be tucked in whatsoever. Occasionally, I get tired of Ron's legs moving in his sleep and walking the blankets and duvet right off the bed at night, so I get up and tuck in the bottom edges of the duvet at night in hopes it will keep it secured to the bed and that I won't have to go searching for covers when I get cold.

The same morning as the laundry sorting, Ron must have been hyper-vigilante and observant. He made the bed and I noticed that it looked awful. He had taken the bottom two corners of the duvet and tucked them in just as I had them the previous night before bed. He's literal and willing. There is never a dull moment!

All I can say is this man keeps trying and he gets an A+ for me because of it. And no, he has not learned to ask if something puzzles him, until it is too late.

Also, Ron wants me to let you know he's become quite proficient at changing faucets, hanging lights, and screwing things into the wall.

One thing we do share is a love of sports: in particular basketball, volleyball, and football. I learned that if I can spout off a few stats to my husband he will open up like a flower. However, what bores me silly is when someone expounds at length on every little detail that quite simply does not interest me. In the next chapter I will share my pain with you and put you through a typical sports conversation, or should I say monologue?

Chapter 13. The language of a Diehard Sports Fan

Sports lingo absolutely confuses me. I do not understand all the *sportisms* I hear people referring to. And yes, I do realize *"sportisms"* is not a real word, but I'm not convinced sports talk is real, either.

Sportisms are love language to the sports fanatic. All I have to say to Ron is "Did you see that assist Terry had to Kidd when he backed it out to the three point line in the game against Miami?" The floodgates open and here is a typical response.

First of all, my lingo evidently did not contain the appropriate sportisms, because Ron is gazing at me with a look that says he's not computing. I can see the gears grinding, he grins, and responds with. "Oh yeah, you mean the dish Terry served Kidd when he shot it back and fired one off from downtown? It was okay, but I think Stevenson moved the screen and Chalmers should have been able to pick that one off but his butter fingers got in the way. The three point shot earlier by the Mavs fell like a brick; it needed more arc; needs some air, you know? At least James had nothing but net on his and drained it although he Gilmored Marion!"

If I were not accustomed to basketball lingo, I would have interpreted the above to mean "Terry gave Kidd a plate, but Kidd threw the plate at him, and then shot at it like when target shooters yell "Pull" and aim at the clay plate. He goes onto say that Stevenson moved the television screen and was judging Chalmers for not picking up the television because he had a candy bar on his fingers. The Mavs three point shot was made with a brick that needed to be blown up with air. At least the deflated brick had a net around it although it went down the drain in the town of Gilmore Marion.

Huh? May be we should try football.

Ron informs me that "Romo fired a desperate Hail Mary at the tight end whose alligator arms failed to secure the leather which still resulted in a blindside hit from the safety who was lurking nearby as the pigskin tumbled harmlessly to the frozen tundra. On the ensuing play, Romo barely avoided a sack while lateraling the skin to the fullback which would have separated his head from his shoulders. On third down, Romo took the team to the line of scrimmage, got the snap, but the lineman jumped across the neutral zone just as the pocket broke down and Romo sailed the ball high over the outstretched arms of his intended receiver as the ball ended up in the arms of the safety as he returned it for a Pick Six in the other direction".

With this narrative, I paused to digest it. I am not great at football terminology because I have a difficult time following the game. To me, this is because the rules are complicated. With much determination I tried to define what he said. Imagine how perplexed I was, because my literal interpretation is:

"Romo took a gun and fired it: someone had to say their Hail Mary's because it was so dangerous. The poor person he aimed at had really dry skin and couldn't protect his leathery skin because they were hit by someone else who was trying to assist them into safety. Then pigs must fly because one landed on the frozen Alaskan ground. Somehow the game goes on and Romo is dodging bags while the pig's skin is on his side: man that could have taken his head right off. But play goes on and after a third try Romo packed up his team and took them for a game of scrimmage, but he snapped and the game piece they called the lineman jumped across the line in the middle of the pool table and the ball went over Romo and to the place it was supposed to go but somehow his arms were safe as he picked the Six ball on the other side of the table." (I'm exhausted!)

I'll give you a couple more examples that may very well start that much needed yawn for you. Ron says, "The way they ran that route sure showed moxy. I mean the meat hook? Come on. The QB was in the pocket! It's too bad they got the death penalty: they could have gone all the way with plays like this." I won't even try to give you a literal interpretation, but it has something to do with gumption and running an assigned play and pool.

Since I obviously don't get football, maybe I'll get volleyball. All of my kids played and they expected me to understand all the euphemisms because of it.

Try following this one about volleyball. When my son speaks, he's generally speaking in context of the setter position. The way I understand the setter position is that they are supposed to get every second ball. The first ball is received by a back row player and the setter gets to the second ball and sets it up to a hitter for the last hit allowed: three hits total. When he describes his games in great detail, it goes something like this. Let's call the opposing team the Eagles.

"The Eagles placed a pipe and over it went right to me for a six pack. If they had just blocked out I wouldn't have had a broken window. That just fired our team up, so our La Barrel got cake enabling the left hitter to get a doughnut D. It was a real Bermuda triangle. So awesome! He is a cleaner, for sure. Boy can he dig! Then it was my go and when the Eagle's middle hitter came at me I roofed him. Everyone in the crowd was yelling "roof, roof". That just pumped us up more. When the score was 22-21, Eagles, they set a brick. It was our turn to serve and it was an Ace; all floor. The score was tied and wouldn't you know, we got a bus stop and then right after that an Oscar. By then it was game point and our back row had a pancake which allowed me to dump it. The Eagles then shanked it and the game was ours."

If you do not follow volleyball then the literal interpretation you are hearing could be this. "The Eagles threw a pipe over me and I won a six pack. If my team had blocked the pipe, they wouldn't have broken the window. The local baker must have been in the stands from the bakery La Barrel, so we got cake and doughnuts which fired us up, or gave us a sugar high. The doughnut was called a Bermuda triangle: I guess because the middle of the donut is lost? Anyway, they were awesome. When he's not playing our back row likes to dig and clean." (Why does he have to throw in these side bars, I'm wondering?) "When it was my turn the Eagle's had a team member in the middle that I beat because I got higher than a house on him. The crowd liked that I got so high over the hitter and kept yelling roof. We were stoked, the game was close. We got to serve because we drew an Ace, the highest card. Right when the score was tied Oscar arrived at the bus stop. It must have distracted the Eagles because the Eagles had a 1 point lead. Wouldn't you know our back row got hungry again so they had a pancake? However, I wanted to finish the game, so I dumped the pancake. The Eagles hit a bar and we won."

Makes no sense, does it? I know I was reaching on that literal interpretation, but let this serve as a reminder to sports enthusiasts. If you have someone included in your conversation who does not closely follow your sport, you may want to use laymen's terms unless it is your goal to disclude that person from said discussion.

I could continue onto baseball, but will spare you. I'll give you one last thought to ponder as you drift off to sleep. Am I the only one who gets grossed out when a player horks a loogie????? Literally, spits? Perhaps I had better give you one more thought. I'd hate to give you nightmares thinking about loogie contests. (Yes, they really do have them). Think adjustment: that'll conjure up a lot of images.

Chapter 14. Adjustments

The word adjustment leaves much to envisage.   Is it an attitude, your spine, your life's purpose, your children, radio station, car engine, clothing alteration, amending a document, altering your medication, finances? The list could go on and on. Permit me to consider several of these with you. I can almost hear you groan. "Perfect! That is just what I want!" Not!

How many times have you heard or said, "You need to adjust your attitude"? This statement is generally met with a negative reaction, often manifested with looking heavenward, rolling of the eyes, lifting of the shoulders, forming a straight line with your lips tightly pressed together, hands shoved in your pockets shaped into fists, toes digging into the carpet, and a snapping up of the head.

You may have followed one or many of those gestures, with the thought "Why is it my attitude that has to change? Isn't it their problem; how they receive the information?" Touchy territory, there, but I have an example for you to illustrate this from.

98

Bored To Sleep

Ron and I were shooting pool in our basement. We had inherited this pool table with the house. Ron grew up with one, but I did not. For him it is like riding a bike: without effort. He literally beats me at a 15:1 ratio. With this in mind, I feel a little bit touchy when we play.

There is a television in the basement great room near our pool table and it is a distraction to my husband. He is one of these men who like watching the commercials maybe even more than the television shows they sponsor.

Last night a movie trailer came up, one we'd previously commented we would like to see. We knew it was coming out on DVD. I spoke up and said:" honey is it the 24ᵗʰ of this month or next month?" Ron's response was, "yes I know, we need to see that!" Huh?

So I say again, "Is it the 24ᵗʰ of this month or next?" Eyes still on the television while sinking the next striped ball in a game of 8 ball, he replies, "I said, we'll need to rent it."

Now, frustrated, I raise my voice to a higher pitch thinking maybe he doesn't have it tuned out at that tonal evel and repeat my question. Response is the same. Now I lose it. "Ron, you aren't listening to me and I'm really offended. I keep asking you the question and you aren't listening to a word I'm saying!"

Eyeing the cue ball, lining his pool stick up with the next shot, he says with an offended tone, "I told you we'll rent it!"

Now I'm really ticked. I reply with a nasty tone, stomp my foot and demand he stop to look at me. It doesn't help that this entire time, I still haven't had a turn while he continues to clear the stripes off the slate. And do you know what????? He is mad at ME! I'm really offended now trying to figure out why in the world I'm on the hot seat. He doesn't like my presentation and I defend myself saying I think he's being disrespectful and making me feel unimportant by giving the television and the pool table more important than my questions.

We're both stubborn, so we turn the TV down, and continue playing the game. Finally I get a turn, but I hit the ball too hard and I scratch. Ron wins and we start a new game. I've got my chin jutted out and a stiff upper lip. He has a pulse throbbing on the side of his neck. He makes the break by hitting the cue ball toward the triangular shape of the balls I racked up for him. Thwack. It hits the balls with authority, they scatter, and go in every direction, AND two stripes full neatly into the pockets.

We finish the game and I say I've had enough pool for one night. Then I remember our motto: never go to bed mad at each other, yet other than his throbbing neck he gives no indication that he is aware I am upset, although I've done my best to make it childishly obvious. So, treating him like the dumb jock I consider him to be at the moment, I look him in the eye and say, "do you realize we're heading up to bed and I'm still very angry with you?"

Ron's response is classic. "Yes I realize that and I was going to talk when we got upstairs." Rebelliously I'm thinking, "Thanks for letting me in on that little secret."

What is the outcome? We both had to use the word "adjustment". We had to step into the other person's shoes, step back and look at ourselves and then adjust our attitude by making concessions. I conceded that my tone would make any man defensive when I got pissy and he conceded that he should have stopped shooting pool and turned from the TV when he realized I asked the same question 3 times. Yes, I agree, if I'm still asking the question,

then that should have been a clue he wasn't listening.
. We made the adjustments and there was peace in our house once again.

Another form of adjustment is an adjustment to the spine. If the spinal cord traveling from the neck to the buttocks (layman terms here) misaligns, then all sorts of other things can go wrong as a result. Problems in the neck can travel down the arm or cause headache. A maladjusted thoracic spine (mid-back) can make it feel as if it is hard to twist and turn or even breathe properly. A misaligned lower spine can cause not only back pain, but tingling in the leg, and foot drop when you walk. There are many ailments one may experience due to a misaligned spine, but the point is; if you are out of alignment, you may need an adjustment.

The frustrating part when it is something stupid that throws the back out in the first place such as a hearty sneeze, cough, sitting down, or pulling something out of a dresser drawer. One time my dad was in need of an adjustment when he leaned under the hood of his car to inspect a spark plug. The need for adjustments can come out of the blue.

Adjustments allow the caregiver to line the discs in your spine back into a neat row of segments, equally spaced and supple. The muscles around the spine help to hold it in place. If you are a neurologist or orthopedist I apologize for the simplistic description.

Sometimes an adjustment is not enough. If the muscles hold a series of spinal segments in place, then those muscles must be exercised and made strong to keep it in place. Just as an attitude had to be adjusted by exercising self-control and the ability to flip the coin, so must a muscle be exercised to hold a new adjustment. (If you think hard enough about this simplistic explanation, I'll just bet it aided you in forgetting whatever it was that is keeping you awake in the first place). Many of the exercises used are called "core" exercises for your back.

What if you gain or lose weight? If you do, then you must adjust certain things such as your clothing. If you gain weight, you must let out the seams and if you lose weight, the seams need to be taken in to make your clothes fit better. Or, you need to adjust your wardrobe by purging your old wardrobe and purchasing a new one which is much more fun. How many people sew these days, anyway? Unless you're Arnie, you may not use a tailor, either.

Unexpected purchases can be an adjustment for those of us on a budget. You may have so much money allotted each month toward clothing and recreation. If your body size has changed and you need more clothing in a particular month, then you must adjust your budget by squeezing another budgeted area. Perhaps you go out to eat a few less times or you buy fewer desserts when grocery shopping, or walk instead of driving to a few nearby functions to save on gas.

Medications can be adjusted. Many people have to return to their physician a few times to have their blood re-tested in order to be certain that they have been given the right level of medication and that it is having its desired effect.

Adjustments require change; moving with the flow even when you may not want to.

A solid understanding of the many types of adjustments can come in handy in the workplace whether as a boss or an employee. Some bosses would do well to consider that maybe it's not the employee who needs an attitude adjustment. If a boss comes into the office with a grumpy demeanor, their staff will pick up on it. If a staff member is brave enough to confront their boss, they must cross their fingers that their boss is fair enough to consider the possibility that they are affecting those around them.

In the next chapter we'll ponder what makes a good boss and employee.

Chapter 15. How to Be a Good Employee and/or Boss

Now that we have established that there are times in life when making adjustments may be necessary, we could apply that to the workplace.

If you are a boss, ask yourself:

Are you a micro-manager helicopter boss, a hands-off boss, a roll up your sleeves boss, or the one who takes credit for what your staff does?

What is a micro-manager? In my world, a micro-manager is one who must have their hands in every aspect of a project no matter how small the detail. They want to control control control and do not trust their staff to have a positive outcome unless they approve every little thing.

You know the type: they are the person in charge who loves to hear themselves talk. They can say in 5000 words what someone else can say in 1000. What I feel is wrong with this is that they lose their audience: not everyone has the attention span to hang onto every last word. The employees lose the point. It's kind of like parenting: your kids lose the point.

Is there a hidden message the employee receives when a boss goes on and on and on? Yes. What they hear is:

"You are not competent: I cannot trust you to do this by yourself, and you are not reliable. You are a kindergartner and not an independent thinker. You do not have an original idea and if you do, then I feel threatened by you. I must take credit for what you do so that <u>my</u> bosses think <u>I'm</u> the one really working hard and earning those high wages."

To be fair, an employee should ask themselves why their boss is micro-managing.

Perhaps it is because upper management or the highest level boss is putting pressure on this employee to accomplish a specific task within a certain budget and a specific timeframe. Since they are in management, maybe they are sworn to protect the head of the corporations' motivations and private discussions.

Or, maybe they're given bonuses based on the outcomes, which ends up being a great part of their salary.

There's always the possibility that the employee(s) really are letting down their end of the work and maybe a sympathetic boss is trying to spare their job by enabling them through micro-managing.

The one motivation I think speaks the most is that the boss whether middle or upper management may be insecure. They are not confident enough to accomplish their goals based on anyone's merit except their own. They have an over-inflated opinion of their value and an under-inflated opinion of their staff.

What makes a good boss? I think it's striking a balance. As a boss you must know your audience, which is your staff. Understand what makes them tick, gets them excited, and show them you value them. Valuing your employee doesn't equal bringing donuts to one of those meetings where you go on and on; instead bring those donuts or something healthier for no reason at all.

Remembering to roll up your sleeves and know how their job works. If you are not afraid to get your hands dirty, then your staff won't be hesitant, either.

Treat them like adults. Have a set of expectations and hold everyone to the same level. Don't sweat the small things like talking for two minutes by the water cooler, but discourage whispering and gossip. Maybe it's just me, but if I hear someone whispering, then I make the assumption I'm not supposed to hear it, so either they are talking about me (paranoia here), or they shouldn't be saying it in the first place.

Because they are adults, include staff in on decisions that directly affect them. Rather than those meetings where they fall asleep to your monologue, make it a dialogue.

I started a monthly brown bag meeting where I provided the food, but everyone participated. The staff was part of the agenda. It was called the "Did You Knows." Each person was responsible for sharing something that pertained to their particular task that would benefit the entire group. They took this very seriously and at future meetings would hold each other accountable for what they brought to the table.

If the environment permits, try tweaking the dress code. See if being casual in dress encourages more productivity or less. My rule was that if the big bosses and customers were not around, then casual was just fine. Modesty was explicitly defined, though, since everyone's interpretation to a rule is subjective. I have seen studies where the more business like the dress, the more business like the attitude. Know your staff. If you have one who is cursed with swollen feet and there isn't an insurance reason against wearing open toed shoes or kicking their shoes off underneath their desks to don slippers; let them. Who is it going to harm? Just make sure they put the slippers or socks on: you don't need others complaining of stinky feet!

If you are the employee, understand that your boss has tasks to complete. They get there in the morning early to catch up on work, but an eager employee may also get there early and decide this is their time to give their list of complaints to the boss. Remember bosses like to keep their doors open and make themselves available to their staff. In order to do this they need boundaries. The boss does not have a target on their back that says "ready, aim, fire!"

Do not adapt the attitude that the rules do not apply to you or that you are the bosses favorite. Those in charge need to protect that privilege and protect the employees from feeling that you have favorites.

Keep it light. If you can play a bit with the employees, it makes the workplace a little less stressful. For instance, each time there was a new staff member; I elicited the aid of my staff to pull a practical joke on the new person. If they are on phones I would crank call them as the most outrageous customer they were like to ever encounter. Once they realized they'd been punked, everyone would gather around, laugh and the employee would immediately feel they were a part of the group.

In a medical office I had a new nurse practitioner who was pretty crusty around the edges. One staff member brought in a dummy that looked like a really creepy life sized clown. We put a hospital gown on it, placed it under a blanket on the examination table and then had her go to the exam room to treat her first patient. Imagine the peals of laughter as expletives came out of her mouth when she pulled back that sheet. Later in her initial week we also transferred a phone call of an employee posing as a patient who claimed they had super glue stuck to their anus, thinking it was their hemorrhoid cream. The results were priceless and paid off for months to come.

April Fool's Day? Don't even get me started. I pulled so many pranks (harmless of course) on my staff over the years. I got away with it for the first 4 years at my last place of business. I just looked so innocent, they had no idea it was me wreaking havoc on them. They finally got even and pulled a fast one on me in exchange; feeling comfortable to do so because they knew I was not a stuffed shirt. Even though I made them feel at ease, it was important to clearly draw the boundaries and be a strong by fair advocate.

The point to this prose is to relax, do not take yourself too seriously and remember it is a gift to lead. Lead with humility and fairness.

If you are a line item employee, have a good attitude: maybe you need to look at the other side and ask yourself why the situation may be as it is.

Occasionally you will have that horrible egotistical boss whose head twists around in a 360 degree circle. In those cases, do not be alone with them, keep a witness, and never let them smell your fear. They are like a shark and will circle in for the kill. Fear can be crippling such as fear of flying.

Chapter 16. Fear of Flying

A frightening boss may be one thing, but what about the fear of flying? For me, flying is one of the top things on my list of things I wish I never had to do. I hope this chapter doesn't stimulate your imagination if you have an overactive one like me. Sometimes simply reading about someone going on and on about their little experiences can be boring as hell and make you check out faster than anything. Maybe I should tell you about my 4 pregnancies and childbirth. (I'm really resisting the temptation to slap a happy face right here.)

Flying is something I cannot control: all I can control is that darned attitude of mine again. You may have experienced some of the same emotions that I have.

In my life I can trace my fear of flying back to an event. In my case, my uncle had a single engine Cessna that he piloted. For my 10th birthday my parents thought they would have him take me and my friend up in the plane for a ride. I don't know why my uncle had a plane or how he got it; I just know I hated it.

These days he would never get away with what he did to us, but back then it was a different world. With my parents out of sight and us in the air, he began to show off and do acrobats. We squealed with terror which fueled his desire to elicit an even stronger reaction from us.

That little red and white plane dove straight for the telephone wires and then pulled back up. We flew upside down and I squeezed my eyes closed. I was sure my life at the tender age of 10 was over. I'm certain it affected me much more than my friend, because she didn't talk about it with the same horror I did.

The last prank he played on us was to say that little planes are much safer than large airliners, because they can glide. To demonstrate, he cut the engine and we caught an updraft of air. He claimed airliners could drop out of the sky like a pancake unlike his little plane. (The following year the co-owner of this plane crashed it: he, his wife, and their 5 year old daughter all were killed). And what did that do? It fed my fear.

Somehow that day we landed and rather than taking away the fact I survived all that in a plane, I left with a permanent terror of flying.

The next time I flew was on a commercial airliner flying from Chicago to Tucson. It did not help that the week before the same type of plane flying out of Chicago on take-off went straight up into the air and then right back down, killing all aboard.

When I'm fearful, I remember all the negative things. I do not contemplate how awesome the last flight was: just like floating on glass, but I remember each flight that had turbulence. Or how we went to Sacramento and didn't even feel a bump.

The clouds look really cool when they float below the plane and the mountains are awesome when topped with snow. Do I appreciate the beauty? Nope: I'm negative Nelly. I mean I've landed in a sudden snowstorm in Baltimore without any issues at all, but just the thought of stopping on a newly snowy runway intimidated the crap out of me. I'm sure the airport had it all under control, but again, my imagination fed my fear.

I have the misfortune of often sitting near the wing more than I would like. I find myself not wanting the window seat because I can see too much that feeds my overactive imagination. I will note the engines and furtively steal glances out the window to make sure there is not fire coming out. If the wing flaps move up and down, I worry that it's unintentional. And if they don't move I worry that they're stuck.

When the landing gear goes up and down, making a screech and a clunk, I'm sure the plane is falling apart, rather than being grateful the plane has landing gear. If I stare at the floor, I think a hole is going to blow in it and suck me out. (I've heard of this happening).

The take-offs really freak me out. I am afraid of flipping over. I've seen news reports where the plane turns too sharply or takes off too steeply and they come to a fiery end. When the engine strains on take-off I think it's going to misfire.

Have you ever flown and the landing was so hard things rolled down the aisles? That happened to me in Europe when my husband was stationed there: the pilot braked so suddenly that all the canned drinks in the back galley flew out of the cupboards and rolled down the aisles. And how did we reward that pilot? We all clapped when the plane came to a halt.

Well done, well done: you scared the crap out of us and now we love you.

I literally had one flight coming home from Las Vegas where we flew through a monsoon storm. The turbulence shook the plane like a tin can. Lightning was flashing outside the windows. Either we were going to burst into thousands of pieces or we were going to be zapped by that lightning. My seatmates were a young married couple. I must have looked extremely panicked, because the lady said to her husband, "I think I need to hold her hand". She took my hand and I let her! I didn't feel embarrassment until we were safely on the ground.

I've also had overhead compartments fly open and bags fall on my head. One time flying to Seattle on take-off on a 115 degree very windy day, the plane literally rocked back and forth dramatically as it taxied down the runway. It continued to rock back and forth wings going up and down as we approached the mountains ahead of us. The plane strained and groaned against the headwind working to get over the mountain. Twice it dropped on an air pocket on take-off. There was a big "oooooh," in unison from all the passengers. I never prayed so hard in my life. A 3 year old boy in the seat ahead of me asked his mom if we were on a roller coaster. Crud! The innocence of a child made me want to weep. If only I could be like him and not have a clue as to what could come next. He had an imagination, too, only he was at an amusement park and I was in hell. These experiences only served to enhance my fear once again.

When friends say to me that "when it's our time to go, it's our time,) I'm not sold. Being the control freak that I am, I want my say in how it happens. I want it to be as non-terrifying as possible.

Add in September 11, 2001 to the mix and I become literally sick when getting on a plane. We lived in England at the time and routinely flew from London to Phoenix to see family. There were army tanks at the London Heathrow airport for crying out loud. From that point on, my fascination graduated from the engines and wings to the other passengers.

I felt it was my civic responsibility to watch each passenger, certain that my plane was the one that does not have an air marshal aboard. Literally two weeks after 9/11 there was a passenger on my overseas plane who got a last minute ticket onto the plane, who dressed and looked like Osama Bin Laden, and who seemed to enjoy the discomfiture he caused the passengers. He literally walked around the plane opening and shutting cupboards, including the flight attendants', looking for a place to hang his robe. After take-off he proceeded to remove his overshirt and stripped down to white boxer-like shorts and a white undershirt. For an older looking guy he was muscular and intimidating. He even flexed his muscles in the aisle, at which time two big guys flanked him to supposedly strike up a conversation. I felt grateful; as if I could relax my guard for a little while. I wasn't profiling, I was just struck with the resemblance to Osama and at his obvious pleasure in making the passengers uncomfortable.

Still, I know my fear of flying is out of balance, so I decided to be proactive and face my fear.

What if I educated myself about flying? Maybe I would believe what people were saying: that it was statistically much safer than a car.

Hence, I signed up for flying lessons. My class, fortunately, didn't make us take ground school simultaneously with air time. In ground school I learned about lift, drag, air pockets, torque, weight, calculating fuel capacity, etc. I also had taken a Meteorology class to understand weather patterns. I stunk at reading maps, though. I do not have navigational skills.

I think you've already figured me out: it did not work. The more I learned about air pockets and the things that could go wrong, the more fearful I became. For the first time in my life, I dropped out of a class.

I just know that people who have been seated next to me on a plane can feel my fear no matter how much I try to act cool. Oddly enough I do much better when my husband is not with me; (minus the stranger hand holding encounter from Las Vegas). When he is next to me, I feel safe to let down and let go. He lets me lean on him and so I don't draw upon my inner strength as readily.

What do I do when all else fails? I call my doctor and say, "I have horrible anxiety, and may I have enough Xanax for just the take-offs on this trip?" It prevents me from having an all-out heart attack and my seat mate doesn't have to hold my hand. In my case, being comatose isn't a bad thing and the people around me appreciate it. I never have taken Xanax for any other thing, so please don't think I'm some kind of drug addict. But, it's okay once in a while to be in charge of not being in charge, if that makes sense.

You were hoping I was off this tangent, but I have one more road to go down: the ill seatmate. If fear of flying isn't enough, I don't like germs, either. Most of us have had the sneezing, snizzling, sniffling, vomiting, and farting passenger nearby.

I was stuck on one of those trans-Atlantic flights next to a guy seated at the window. Shortly after take-off he promptly got up and vomited in a bag on his way down the aisle to the bathroom. Some overflow dropped onto his shirt. He did not have a spare shirt. Additionally, he needed the aisle seat where I was still watching for terrorists, so I had to reluctantly take his germy window seat. It smelled so bad. Thankfully the girl in the middle seat had a swab of green tea perfume. We went to the back of the plane, rubbed it on our wrists and would surreptitiously smell our wrists throughout the flight when it got to be too nauseating. After that nauseating 11 hour trip, I learned to keep a spare shirt in my carry on to either change into or to offer up to the person next to me who still smelled like barf!

Don't get me started on farts: the kind my family member sneaks out on an airplane; a silent but deadly (SBD) fart. In his case, it sat in a cloud right over our heads and remained there. I made exaggerated outrageous offended faces at him so everyone else around us with eyes watering knew it WAS NOT ME!

What is it about farting, anyway?

Chapter 17: Flatulence

Oh, the "F" word! True story: a friend whose son was in kindergarten at a Christian school told me the Kindergarten teacher said to her in a hushed voice "I need to speak to you about your son after school today. He said a bad word."

"What? He did? I'm confused: we don't say bad words at our house."

The teacher replied, "I'll talk to you about it after class today."

My friend was on pins and needles all day: her husband was the assistant principal of this school and she couldn't imagine how the gossip mill would love to find out about her son's misdeeds. (Yes, I hear what you're thinking: who cares and for crying out loud, he's 5 years old: get a grip, but…..)

School dismissed and she reluctantly approached the teacher, having run all imaginable scenarios through her mind without being any closer to an explanation.

"Mrs. Nystadter, what did my son say?"

Mrs. Nystadter pursed her lips, drew a deep breath, and stated, "He said the "F" word.

"The **F**- Word? He's never heard that in our house; I can assure you!" My friend was devastated.

Mrs. Nystadter proceeded. "Yes, he said (slight pause)----*fart!*".

Before she could stop herself, my friend said "Fart? He said fart? That's it?" Remembering her audience, she showed the appropriate respect for the elder Mrs. Nystadter's sensibilities and promised she would speak to her little boy.

In my house, we weren't allowed to say fart, either. It was known as "passing gas". To me that is much more graphic. Yuck! Gas? Ewwwww.

My mom would be in the hated fabric store, pull out a fabric end from a bolt and study it while confessing she just passed gas. I would make a mad dash for another row; bury my head in the scent of new fabric, embarrassed beyond belief.

The other memorable place she would "pass gas" was in the ladies dressing room. I was a captive audience there and could not escape. There were no bolts of fabric to bury my face in.

What about the slow release flatulencer? (yes the word is yet another KC-ism). I was in a grocery store aisle one day and a little old lady carefully bent over slowly reaching down to the canned goods on the bottom shelf. I was not in time to assist her. The entire way down a whoosh of air was audibly being released. It was not loud; just a slow burn. She either couldn't hear herself or had reached the point where she just didn't care. She had earned the right to fart.

Others guilty of slow release flatulence are the ones who think if they release it in stages, no one will hear, smell, or notice the content look on their faces.

Have you ever been in a meeting and your bowel started rumbling? It starts like a slow grumbling, but is in the nether regions. When I was in a board meeting (full of surgeons, mind you; who regularly listen for bowel sounds), my bowel started rumbling. I patted my stomach and whispered to it, oh stop growling: dinner will be soon. I often wondered if I actually fooled them. What I needed to do was excuse myself from the room and find a place far enough away from their ears. These rumbling farts are the ones that are explosive. In fact, I left the building figuring I was only safe in the parking lot.

How about the people who "let-em rip"? They are the ones who think it is a challenge to produce a disgusting odor. They rip ones with a capital R. Who better than my firefighter ex-husband? At the firehouse it was considered an honor to have the most disgusting aroma possible. The firefighters would have contests. I like to tell myself they must have been bored and were hoping to light a match and create a fire to fight just for something to do. Some of those rips should have been considered a potential for arson!

Let me be the first to inform you that I am not a public flatulence releaser. I am blushing as I type this chapter: really! To me the big D (Diarrhea) and gaseous smells are something better left unsaid. I mean, honestly: the way I see it, won't my man see me as nauseating as the smell coming from my hindquarters? (Deep purple blush here).

Well, I have only had two times in my past where I was let's say; busted, if you don't count the grumbling bowel sounds in that meeting).

The first time was when I was 16 years old and hoping to impress a 20 year old guy I was crushing on. We were ice skating with a group of high school and college kids on a frozen river. Sitting on a tree stump, riverside, I lifted my leg to lace my ice skates and one escaped. He was only arm lengths away. A 14 year old boy immediately remarked, "You just cut one!" And to my chagrin, my crush heard it, because he reprimanded the boy and told him to stop. Any ideas I had of being cool and flirtatious flew away along with my gas, not to mention my confidence!

Now fast forward to my ex-husband. I never ever ever ripped one in front of him. At the time I was 8 ½ months pregnant with our first baby. We were shopping for a crib. When I squatted down to view bedding, a loud explosion escaped from between my buttocks: I literally think my butt cheeks vibrated! Well, not only did my ex hear, but he hooted in laughter. In fact it was so funny to him that he couldn't stop slapping his thigh. Ultimately he collapsed on his knees to the floor, still snorting and laughing all the while pointing at me and saying "you farted! You farted!"

At this point, people were beginning to turn their attention to the commotion in aisle 3. I struggled back into an upright position, smoothed my maternity shirt down over my voluminous belly, stuck my nose up in the air, and marched out the doors without looking back. I may have not seen him as I exited, but I could still hear him roaring with laughter!

Ironically, that precious baby girl I gave birth to ended up being just like her dad: a public belcher and emitter of gas, and proud of it! I call her my delicate little flower.

But, you haven't met another one of my daughters. I have three daughters, actually, and one son. They are content to share their bowel stories with each other and have no qualms about sharing this with the rest of the family and close friends.

My daughter, we'll call her Janey, and my second daughter, we'll call Sharon, have the most sensitive noses known to mankind. They are the inventers of the imagined fart. They are always saying to whoever is unfortunate enough to be in the vicinity of their identified fart aroma, "you farted!" When it is aimed at me, I am mortified, because I know it's not true. The more I deny, the more they insist it was me. I know I replied with the quip "Whoever dealt it smelt it"!

One time they accused the room: "Someone farted". Their stepmom, a meek and mild woman, quietly spoke up and said, "It was me." I was aghast! How could she own it? How embarrassing! My girls were worse than crotch sniffing dogs.

My son-in-law comes up with scientific theories as to why my daughter shouldn't share her farts with him. His science is his defense mechanism against his wife's locker room antics.

His theory is this: The skin is an organ, and when someone farts, the odor is absorbed by the skin. It therefore is not fair to share your fart with others, because then they will smell like it, which is what makes it rude. He explains that is it no different than walking into a room with smokers: when you leave the room, you wreak like tobacco. Or, if you eat garlic you smell like it: it releases from your pores.

How in the world do you argue with this? Anyone guilty of making my son-in-law smell farts will be given the lecture. I don't want to be on the receiving end of said lecture.

Do you remember my employer, Dr. Arnie? He was truly the first to make my eyes water from the silent but deadlies: SBD. But then again, I had not met my current husband, Ron, yet. Ron is the king. Unlike my ex, Ron isn't proud of the gas, he just can't control it. He is the non-claimant. That is why he must sneak out a silent fart. He usually blames it on something he ate such as beans or dairy products. Finally this year I decided to play his game, so I bought Almond Milk. I guess time will tell if that works. He says Gas-Ex doesn't work, so at this point it's time to embrace the SBDs. It does kind of ruin my desire for deviled eggs, though.

Non-claimants are fidgeters. They squirm, shift back and forth in their seat, pull their legs together at the knees, and squeeze their butt cheeks. The squeeze is their downfall. Their SBD is released into the air: the non-circulating, stale airline type air.

Last, I would be remiss if I did not mention a colo-rectal surgeon I worked with. He was an extremely difficult physician to work for and all employees agreed he was in the right line of work since we all felt like we'd had our share of ass chewing when around him. He loved working with the colon, large intestine, small intestine, and rectum. (I'm blushing again, by the way).

One time during a training session with him, an emboldened employee asked if the gas patients released during procedures were off putting. He replied with, "The human plumbing is astounding and fascinating".

I decided right then something wasn't quite right: we're plumbing? So, those farts are just our bodies flushing and the odors are what come out of our sewer? Ick! He said the sphincter muscle, (which releases things), can be triggered by something as simple as chewing a piece of gum: many patients have different triggers. I was taking mental notes, hoping to find the secret to keeping farts completely to myself. I have to admit, he was great at his specialty and so knowledgeable.

He was very gifted as a surgeon and his patients loved him. The staff ended up referring to him as "AW"; the Ass Whisperer. He just retired and has no idea of the love name bestowed upon him.

So, we end our chapter on flatulence with a light airy note; pun intended.

You know what else is airy? The flight of birds.

Chapter 18. Birds

I would like to share with you my experiences with birds.

Some of you reading this are certain to be dedicated bird lovers, some of you may be indifferent, while others like me, have been damaged by a few negative experiences.

Ah, the beauty of the winged creatures in flight: Capturing the currents, floating, gliding, and diving throughout the landscape. Coupled with their singsong melodies, what could be more wonderful?

They are stunning in flight: a fete I often wished to emulate as a little kid when I would jump off the front porch into the evergreen bushes below, wildly flapping my arms, sure I would eventually fly. I think I spent one summer permanently scraped up from those bushes that captured my every landing.

I have lived in many places, such as Arizona, New Mexico, Illinois, Washington DC, and Oxford, England. Each place offers a variety of birds to admire.

My foibles were formed in childhood as more than likely is your case, too. I have anxieties with winged species due to negative childhood experiences. Winged things: birds and planes. And if you think I'm afraid of everything; you're wrong. I am not bothered by insects.

Joe the Crow was my uncle's pet crow. My uncle was a teen when I was a tot, so he was still living at home. My grandparents lived on a farm. To keep track of me as a toddler, even at ages 3 and 4, my grandma would put me in a big wooden playpen placed strategically on the front lawn outside the kitchen window.

Well, Joe being the smart bird that he was saw that he had a captive audience. He would land on my head; dig his claws into my scalp to hang on while I screamed bloody murder! And believe me I could scream! Evidently he thought this was great sport, because the more I screamed, the more he perched and cawed.

Have you ever been in the vicinity of an unknown birds nest? The kind where you innocently walk outside to a shed to get the lawnmower and a bird flies out at your head?

What about birds in the house? One time I was babysitting my young cousins and their parakeet got out of the cage. I was beyond petrified. I locked

133

the girls in the master bedroom with me and dialed their maternal grandfather. He had to drop everything and come over to cage the parakeet. He was not happy! My aunt and uncle never asked me to babysit again. So, if you want to get out of babysitting, let the parakeet out, lock yourself in a room and cry for help.

Or, the bird that perches on the chimney to get warm in the wintertime and falls in? This happened to me in a house that had a basement with a big octopus furnace which was severely in need of an upgrade. You know the kind: they're huge monsters with arms that branch off from the main furnace in those old historic homes. (*Old, historic*; UT-oh, is that redundant?)

The basement steps were located off the kitchen. I still remember opening the basement door to go downstairs and a bird flying into my face as it came up from the basement. You don't forget things like that. And guess what? I had one daughter at the time; she and I hid in the bathroom while the cat chased a screeching bird around the house. I didn't have a cell phone then, so my daughter and I sang songs at the tops of our lungs to cover the noise until my husband got home. Thankfully that was only 20 minutes later. The bird survived and I was left to clean up the droppings. It found a hanging plant of mine and must have hidden in there because there were a lot of white spots. I knew I needed to empower myself and learn how to handle this, but I wasn't past the fear yet.

Another time, same house, I went into the kitchen and opened the microwave oven. It was on the counter below a window. A bird flew out of the window toward my head. This time my husband was home and he chased it outside. By then, I was desperate and so was he. So, the chimney got a screen over it and all was well again. My cure: be proactive!

When I moved to Arizona, the house I lived in had a covered back patio with sliding doors exiting onto it. A Swallow decided to nest above the doors. Each time we opened the doors; it flew at us and would nearly get in the house. The Barn Swallow was very aggressive.

The first time I went to Sea World, a Seagull swooped down at the tray the guy in the food line ahead of me was holding, and knocked it out of his hands and stole his hotdog. I was thankful it wasn't me! But the day wasn't over; during one of the shows while seated in the audience, a Seagull bombed me on the arm. Thankfully I had a sweatshirt on, so I rolled the bird poop up in the sleeve.

I can't tell you how many times as a kid in Illinois when the really cool bird formations would fly over, I got pooped on. We used to yell, "Bombs; run for cover!"

Yes the formations are really cool and being the open minded adult I now am, I have decided that as long as birds are in their own environment, I have nothing to fear. Being an Air Force wife, I often wondered if pilots learned a lot about air formations by watching the birds: some of the air shows we saw certainly resembled the birds flying over my childhood home.

When we lived in England, the birds got into the eaves by removing the screens covering them in the overhang outside. They would nest up in the attic and we would be awakened each morning with the sounds of a dozen birds flying back and forth up there. They made a huge racket. We weren't allowed to do anything about it until nesting season was over. Then we would plug the holes and hope they didn't return. I was so afraid they were going to find their way into the main house. That was one attic that never had a single item stored in it!

Last year I was cutting the grass in our backyard. It is wide open; no trees or anything around where I was. Out of nowhere, birds began diving toward me: I'm talking maybe 12 or more. I never saw them before and I haven't seen them since. I don't know what type they were; I only know they wanted me. Four of the birds began circling me and the lawnmower, making a game out of diving down to the mower, touching it, then circling me. Each time I tried to back up with the mower, they nearly hit me. I could literally touch them. I was panicked like I haven't been in a long time. We live on a corner and do not have a fence: the yard is in full view of any neighbor deciding to watch.

I was trying to be cool and I literally kept mowing with the birds coming at me for a solid 10 minutes, sure they'd go away and that they wouldn't hit me. Well, the longer I was out there, the numbers increased, and the more I was being swarmed. It must have looked hilarious to observers, because I was going fast, then slow, ducking, backing, dodging and moving my arms around me. Finally, I didn't care if I wasn't cool anymore; I hurriedly pushed the mower to the front yard where they proceeded to follow me. I let myself into the garage and hid for about 2-3 minutes. I was so sure they'd follow me into the garage that I only raised it 3 feet and I nearly crawled inside. While inside, I shed my purpled hooded sweatshirt because it was hot in there.

When I returned outside without the sweatshirt, they all lost interest and went away. A coincidence? I don't know, but what I do know is that I won't cut the grass with that sweatshirt on again. I haven't researched it, but could it have been Purple Martins? Maybe their name is "purple" because they're attracted to purple? I was never bothered by birds again when cutting the grass without purple.

Do any of you have parrots or pet birds that are free to roam your homes? I don't! But my aunt does. She has cockatiels and parrots. Her one parrot Chrissy bird used to sit on the tank vacuum cleaner and vocalize, flapping her wings and singing, oh ee ah ee oooh ee ah ee oh! (Did that bird know my mom?)

If my aunt took a shower, that darned bird would walk back and forth on the shower door top. She liked to capture the mist, causing her wings to get wet. My aunt would blow dry her feathers after her shower and Chrissy would vocalize some more.

Yes, birds can be very entertaining. Parrots are hilarious when they mimic their owners. They get the exact tonal quality of the family members and their favorite sayings. If you don't know someone has a parrot and you hear the ruckus from their yelling, you might think your neighbors are really weird or loud. Chrissy would yelp "Moooom, Moooom, Maaaaaa" whenever my aunt covered her cage. My cousin, Paula, was a teenager and Chrissy had my aunt and cousin's voices down to a "T". Chrissy would often perch and say "Paula?" "WHAT!" If the doorbell rang, Chrissy would yell "Hello, Hello, Hello" in my aunt's voice. First time visitors must have thought my aunt was super excited to have company.

This will be my final story on birds. (Your eyes are getting heavy; you are feeling sleepy as you read this, I hope).

My good friend babysits cockatiels for a coworker. (If you read my book "The Corn Stalker", she is the character Teena. If you're familiar with her you'll recall how she marches to the beat of her own drum. A couple weeks ago she thought she'd put the pair of them in the hood of her sweatshirt and go to her favorite local coffee shop. While in there, one of the birds flew out while frightening the patrons. Believe it or not, my friend was surprised they didn't stay put in her hoody. My reaction was strong. I was so thankful I was not there! She is definitely a bird lover so she did not stop to consider the reaction of others. I never did ask what the café owner may have said to her.

Sometimes we just do stupid things.

Speaking of stupid things…..in the next chapter we'll ask a question; maybe even a stupid question!

Chapter 19: Stupid Questions

Is there such a thing as a stupid question? Couldn't that in and of itself be considered stupid?

Have you ever taken a class and noticed that the room seems to be divided into three categories?

1.   The perpetual question asker: the one who keeps you there late. We all want to tell them to shut up, but we're too polite.

2.   The midline questioner: only ask when necessary.

3.   The never question questioner suck it up person.

The perpetual questioners are not self-conscious at all about what they are asking. If they are curious, they are going to make sure they can obtain an answer. They are extroverts.

The mid-liners seem to be more efficient. They are on a need to know basis. Their motivation to ask a question may be simply to spark a conversation and make the classroom time more interesting, giving the instructor a much needed lift. The pleasers!

The never questioners is where I fall, much to my detriment. Even if I need to know, I don't ask. Since this category directly affects me, I thought we could explore it together and analyze our psyche.

What could be the reasons for not asking a question in class? Lying awake pondering this non-life threatening category, I decided it is the following:

1.   The person is extremely intelligent and knows more than the teacher.

2.   Said student is insecure and doesn't want to have the classroom attention focused on him/her.

3.   The student is afraid of asking the stupid question.

4.   The student is an introvert.

So, you're trying to figure out which one you are, not to mention the author of this weird discussion. I would say #1 and #2 are pretty clear and I'm culpable on both. #3 and 4, however, are a bit more complex. If there is fear of asking the stupid question, then chances are, a past experience formulated this viewpoint at some time in the past.

I am guilty of #3 and 4, too. I've had experiences highlighting this with bosses. You know the type: The highly respected well educated individuals, some who may be certifiable geniuses, thus making it more intimidating to ask the stupid question!

When I asked questions at the meetings to gain a better understanding of what was required of me, I would feel the repercussions before the question was even answered. The chair would hurriedly brush over my question as if flicking off a fly. The big boss would say two words which would slice me to shreds while managing to let me know he did not appreciate my thinking outside the box. At least that's how I perceived it: I'm sure they didn't see it that way at all.

"Why?" I would ask myself. At the time I wouldn't have the answer: I would sit in my chair trying not to feel humiliated in front of the others and striving to keep my face from turning red.

When I would go home, lie in bed, and filter, the answer would become more clear. My point/question was valid and I stepped on toes: the question may have seemed like I was throwing them under the bus rather than thinking outside the box.

What message did I get from asking the perceived stupid question? What I heard was shut-up and listen: you are there only because we want you there and we can just as easily uninvited you. I was to be an observer, not a participant. Too bad there isn't a code book for who considers questions to be frivolous versus those who consider them to be enriching.

Still, there are times when a question must be asked, even in a hostile environment. At those times, I consider my question before voicing it, rehearsing a precise short question that will be acceptable in the room. Sad!

There are those who begin a class with, "there is no such thing as a stupid question." I appreciate these people because it puts someone who is anxious at ease. It is a two-edged sword, though. This type of environment enables the perpetual questioner.

To those who do not ever ask questions, remember one thing. Sometimes the teacher, trainer, professor, speaker, whoever is leading, appreciates a legitimate question. It gets the creative juices flowing for the rest of the room, and chances are someone else shares the same question. I can't tell you how many times I was grateful someone asked exactly what I was wondering.

I wonder about a lot of things and question everything in my mind. Here's a stupid question: what about a raindrop?

Chapter 20. Raindrops

This is a very non-scientific, imaginary discussion, only, of the cycle of a raindrop. It is meant to be fanciful, in keeping with the focus of this book.

For those of you who possess literal minds, you may find this chapter offensive. I apologize in advance! (Do you sense insincerity in my apology?)

I have been focused on raindrops for two reasons.

#1. I lived in the desert for far too long, so they are a novelty to me.

#2. I moved to the Midwest to see rain and now we have the longest standing drought much to my bitter disappointment.

The raindrop eludes me and with it the formation of a raindrop.

While trying to will myself to sleep, I find myself turning the question of the raindrop over in my mind. Allowing me to focus on one topic can sometimes invite sleep more rapidly.

The raindrop can be large, small, cause a splatter pattern, drip, spittle, or roll. What's more, a raindrop can be annoying, soothing, insistent, or silent.

Don't you find it fascinating when you're driving in your car and out of the blue, (literally), one big splotch lands on your windshield? Then another, and another, until your car window is dotted with these large splotches.

When I'm a passenger, I'll fixate on those splotches, comparing them to see if the splash pattern is different on all of them, as snowflakes are all unique.

While I'm studying the patterns, a nucleus of the raindrop begins to be weighted by gravity. The force pulls the splatter downwards, creating a raindrop that slowly rolls down out of sight, or if driving fast, is pulled sideways by the wind.

The large splotch is my favorite type of raindrop. When followed rapidly one after another, the sound is amazing. It taps on the windshield and the car roof.

Have you ever been inside the house when these large drops fall and hear them only because they are landing on a sunroof? It is a pitter patter sound:

rhythmic pulsating beats. Love it! Relax, and think about this sound: it'll self soothe you.

My favorite place to be during a rainstorm is in a metal roofed building, such as a cabin. The tinny sound vibrates with hard rainfalls and hail. Some of you may find that sound a violation of your sensibilities: more harsh than peaceful. For me, I feel cocooned in the cabin, safe from the onslaught outside.

What I do not like is being caught in the car when it is a torrential rainfall: unable to see the road ahead, much less analyze drop patterns.

Additionally, when I lived in England, we had spittle rain. Spittle rain is barely a mist, not a sprinkle, but as if the heavens are only spitting. It is just enough to smudge the windshield and force the driver to give the windshield one swipe with the wipers.

The spittle continues without any predictability and the following swipes of the blades create friction: not wet enough to wipe clean, and enough of a nuisance to impair vision; particularly if your windshield was dirty to begin with. You do not want to run out of windshield washer fluid when driving in spittle rain.

Bored To Sleep

Many of you may prefer the raindrop that is small, rolling, and measures out a regular beat, perhaps accompanied by distant thunder. Depending on where you live will more than likely shape your preferences for the raindrop and the background sounds that complement it.

I've heard of tortures provided with the constant drip of water with the express intent of grating on the nerves of the victim. Is it a kind of noise warfare perhaps?

Last, I must say I do enjoy thunder with my large splotchy raindrops. Not loud frightening scary thunder, but rolling thunder. The kind that has me counting one one thousandth, two one thousandths, three one thousandths; boom! I reassure myself with the adage that each second is equal to the lightning being one mile away. The thunder resembles a drummer, slowly drumming out the beats, gaining momentum and hitting a crescendo with the impact of the thunderclap.

Picture this, let go, and go to sleep. Forget about everything; work, home, relationships, meal planning, and your schedule; just let go and forget!

Chapter 21. Forgetfulness

Do any of you remember having a Mom, teacher, or friend tie a string around your finger? It was meant to prompt you to remember whatever it was you might forget? You would wave your hand, see the string, and say "Oh yes, I'm supposed to remember….." Unless as with some people, you look at the string and can't recall what it is you were wearing that darned string for.

Earlier in this book I discussed Dr. Arnie. One time he was seeing an Alzheimer's patient. He had put her in an arm cast (again). She had a habit of looking at the cast on her arm and was always surprised to see it. Upon her discovery of the cast, she would proceed to tear at it and pick it off her arm, bit by bit. Then, her caregiver would have her at our office for repair/replacement.

Finally Doctor Arnie had enough of her forgetfulness, so he pulled a felt tipped purple surgical marker out of his white coat pocket and wrote on her cast in large capital letters, "DO NOT REMOVE: GO TO DOCTOR ARNIE ON AUGUST

21ST WITH QUESTIONS." He even wrote his phone number on there.

Miraculously it worked! Her "bow" had instructions. The ironic part was that later when Doctor Arnie was in his office dictating his office visit notes, he couldn't remember her name so he yelled into my office "KC, what was the name of that patient?"

If only it were that easy when we have memory lapses. We all have word recall difficulties at one time or another and sometimes that includes forgetting people's names.

My husband is famous for running into someone at the store from his workplace and not recalling their name. I will stand by dumbly while he carries on a stilted conversation, obviously working hard to file through his brain for their name. All the while, it is awkward, because introductions have not been made. I now come to his rescue by sticking my hand out and saying hi, I'm KC and you are again?" Even though it embarrasses my husband, it acknowledges the elephant in the room. It's better than thinking it is the stupid question, right?

However, when I am the one who is failing to draw a name out of my mind, I will use creative ways for name discovery.

I have become a master at the elusive name fish. "Hi there (who is he again?), how is your other half?" At this point I'm hopeful he'll say her name in reply. Sometimes I'll address them as "Hey there!" when noticing their presence. If someone who knows them is standing around in a group setting, I may learn over and whisper, "Who is that?"

Other times, I'll do the honest approach and say, "I am so sorry: for some reason I can't recall your name: what is it again?" (See, I can't expect my husband to do that and not be willing to do the same). The honest approach is generally the most appreciated way to do it, as I'm sure people can clearly see I've lost their name and am too proud to ask.

What about movie stars and television actors and actresses? So many times I'll be describing a movie I saw and when asked who was in it, I'll go blank. It's as if someone came along with a giant eraser and wiped it from my memory. This is when the game of charades begins. I'll begin by mimicking what their character did, (because I've forgotten the name of the movie, too), and give some kind of random description such as, "you know, they're middle-aged, maybe 40-ish, hair graying at the temples, always perfect, speaks with a drawl, and you never see his character in anything other than cowboy boots and torn jeans. Oh, and he has a really great walk." The person listening begins to yell out names like "John Travolta" while I shake my head to the negative. It is so upsetting when I lose these words. And, it never fails; the word will come to me once I dismiss the subject and no longer stress to bring it back to the forefront of my mind. You insomniacs know what I'm talking about, because it will compute once you're in bed, trying to relax. You find yourself yelling out the word, enormously proud, while your significant other is looking at you as if you've lost your marbles!

I am positive we all do the march down the hall with determination. We are on a mission. When we get to a room with clear intent, we begin to look around. "Why am I here? What did I want? I know it was something because my stride was so sure." The gaze around begins. You begin to circle the room with your eyes, taking in every last detail, hoping something will jog your memory, and nada; nothing!

What do you do next? You retrace your steps back down the hall. Sometimes you'll get only halfway back and the objective snaps right back into your bean. At other times, you'll get back to your point of origin and do the glance around again. Almost always, it works and your memory is jogged.

We had a neighbor in Tucson who suffered from Alzheimer's. He was not yet in the advanced stages. His name was Jack and Jack liked to take walks every day. Sometimes we would find him with his walker in the middle of the curvy neighborhood road, which did not have sidewalks. We would engage him in conversation while leading him toward the side of the road and back toward his house. In order not to embarrass him, we made it seem natural. Jack had a hobby which was taking pictures of the homes in the neighborhood. While on his walks, he liked to knock on neighbors' doors and offer them a picture of their house. He had a favorite one of ours: it was a picture of it with a rainbow behind the house after a rare thunderstorm.

If you ever saw the movie "Fifty First Dates" with Drew Barrymore and Adam Sandler, you might recall the character *10 Second Tom*. This character's memory lasted 10 seconds and every 10 seconds he would stick out his hand and affably introduce himself. "Hi, I'm Tom". Well, back to our neighbor Jack. Each time he saw us out on one of his walks he would reintroduce himself. When we would walk him back to his house we would watch our clocks, because invariably within 10 minutes he'd be at the door with a picture of our house. We decided to name him *10 Minute Jack*. Finally after many episodes like that we got smart and did not accept the photo. Instead, we took a leaf out of Doctor Arnie's book and wrote our names on it with our phone number. It helped him remember at some point that he must have met us and that we had a picture. I think we wrote something like "thanks for the other pictures" right on the back of it. His wife assisted us and put it on the refrigerator where she encouraged him to write the names of other names on their photos as well. It worked!

Focus is what I often need. When I play against my husband in tennis, I'll announce the score before I serve: he'll respond with 'No that's not it, I have that last point", while I struggle to recall what the last play even was. Recently Diana Nyad set the record for the first person to swim from Cuba to the Florida coast without a shark cage. She's in her 60s and has tried this several times unsuccessfully, beginning in her 20s. When asked by a reporter how she was able to accomplish it now when she was so much older, she quickly responded with "Focus; I am not as fast as I was when I was younger, but I now have the ability to focus."

Whenever we have deficiencies, we learn to cope with them, right? For me, I have repeatedly circled back to Doctor Arnie and his purple pen. I will leave myself a reminder, and in these times of technology it is generally on my preferred electronic method of communication. Now, I just can't lose that item! And, I must focus more. My daughter told me I don't focus because I don't want to. So I choose to want to!

Chapter 22. The Safe Place- Sleepwalker

I'm fairly certain you could see this topic coming. How many of you have that safe place where you have put an item for safe keeping? The weird thing is, the items seem to dissipate into thin air. I will have the memory of thinking "Oh, this is a good place: I'll never lose it here and no one will find it, either." Then, even when the house is sold, packed up, everything is moved and I do a walk through, the item still has not surfaced. How can that be?

I have a theory about this. I think that I dream I saved the item but in reality I was sleep-walking and placed it in the trash bin. (I have found missing silverware in the trash bin many times.)

Have you ever encountered someone who sleep walks or are yourself one who suffers from this malady?

Sleep walking is not to be confused with distracted walking. Distracted walking is the epidemic taking place when cell phone users are pre-occupied with their Smart Phones by either texting, conversing, emailing, face-booking, or playing any number of their applications. This kind of distracted walking has dramatically increased the number of pedestrians struck by motorists.

Sleeping walking occurs in a semi-conscious state. For me, I do not recall when I sleep walk, although I am told some people do have fuzzy recollection. Sleep walkers undertake low functioning tasks while actually asleep. They may do anything such as go to the bathroom, cook a meal, carry on a conversation with people in another room, or in extreme cases, drive a car, have sex with strangers, or worse.

My daughter would get up out of bed, walk in circles, and return to her room. There were times when family was visiting that she would head to the living room where they were camping out, turn on the television and then sit on top of them as if they were the couch.

I am not certain I suffer from sleep walking. My only hint is all of the missing items that I have. When I really am searching for a safe place, I make a mental note on where I put it. I use my focus. When I have no recollection, I can only assume the item was on my subconscious mind and that I got up to place it in a secure location.

I wish it were something like money: how fun that would be to stick my hand in the pocket of my jeans and pull out a $20. That doesn't happen in my world. Money always lands in the land of "safe places."

Some people who sleep walk think they had a graphic dream. When they awaken, the dream is barely on the peripheral of their consciousness and never occurs to them unless something untoward happens. Let me illustrate.

I have had four kids. Whenever I'm in my 7th month of pregnancy, weird behavior temporarily settles in. For me, it is the known cases I have of sleep walking.

I have always liked cats. To those of you cat haters, bear with me: it's worth the read and could be all the more entertaining to you.

My cats before childbirth were my babies. I have never in my life had anything other than a pampered housecat. I am fastidious about making sure everyone keeps outside doors closed, that strangers know I keep the cats inside, and that they aren't put at any unnecessary risk. Equally, I am a dog person, expecting my dog to be a cat lover. This has never been a problem for me; in fact, cats would rule the dogs in our household. I have had a Labrador mix backed into a corner with one stern look from the cat.

One morning in my 7th month of pregnancy, I woke up to feed the cat and couldn't find him. I looked around for him, but got distracted by other duties, and forgot about him for a while. I fed the dog, cleaned up the dog poop, got meat out of the freezer, and headed to work.

When I got home that night, my husband asked me if I'd seen Thumper (the cat). I thought for a minute and said, "No-ooooo, but come to think of it, I did have a strange dream about him last night." Curious, my husband prodded me to continue. "I dreamt that I had to take the trash out when the dog had to go to the bathroom last night. I threw the trash out with the dog onto the back porch." My husband said, "What trash? I took the trash out last night before bed!" Troubled, I replied, "You did? Are you sure?" And then, "UT-oh, I remember in my dream that I thought about Fred Flintstone when the cat threw him out of the front door, turned off the light, all the while Fred is pounding on the door to let him

in: you know, like he was saying "I'm not the trash!"
As I'm saying this, the light is slowly coming on in
my brain. I realize that the "trash" was our cat,
Thumper. I threw the cat outside with the dog.

Three months later, we had moved out of the
house, unsuccessful in our attempts to find Thumper.
We had informed all the neighbors and given them
our forwarding numbers.

One day a week after we had moved a
skeleton of a cat stumbled into our old yard. The
neighbor called us, we drove right over, and it was
Thumper. It was horrible. He weighed 2 pounds and
could barely stand up. (He had been 18 pounds when
I threw him out.) We had a huge vet bill that week.
We had taken him straight to emergency where they
struggled to get IV's connected and rehydrate him.

That cat ended up weighing more than his
previous 18 pound: he had developed an insatiable
appetite. It took me the longest time to get over my
guilt. My only excuse? I had sleep walked.

Have you ever dreamt you had to go to the
bathroom really bad? In the dream, you have to go,
but there's no bathroom within sight. So, you end up
holding it, miserable because the urge is strong.
Somehow, though, you find a rest room and relieve

yourself and it feels so good. When you wake up, it is with relief that you find out it was only a dream, but that you actually do have to urinate, and you make your way to the bathroom, thankful you didn't actually "go" while you were dreaming.

But what about when you're 7 months pregnant and you have that dream? Only when you wake up, you find that along with that nice released state, the bed around you is unusually warm. Imagine how horrified I was when I was that pregnant woman and had to wake up my husband and ask him to get out of bed while I changed the sheets. Even worse, he keeled over laughing just as he did when I farted in the store.

Okay, okay, I confess: it happened one other time and I can't blame it on pregnancy. I was camping with my in a tent beside a rapidly running creek. I was holding "it" in my sleep, while dreaming about black bears, coyotes, and mountain lions. Once again, I awakened to that warm sensation, only there were no sheets to change and only a steamy sleeping bag to throw out the flap while my humiliation seeped in and any remnants of my dignity fled.

That night much to my irritation there was nowhere to hide: no safe place for me!

Sometimes the only safe place to hide is through music.

Chapter 23. Musical Ability

Some say "either you have it or you don't". I disagree. There are many musicians who worked diligently at perfecting their craft. It didn't come naturally, so they practiced for hours on end day after day. Others had a natural ability, flair, or an ear for music and picked it right up with minimal effort in comparison.

I heard a statistic once that said only 15% of pianists have a natural ability for it. In a way, I do understand what the statisticians are saying, even though there's an argument to be had for natural ability versus a lot of hard work.

My piano teacher worked with me from age 6 -14. I could read any music set in front of me. If I got a new music book, I would take it home and play through the entire ensemble, beginning to end: flawlessly. Did I have the "flair" for music? Absolutely not! To me it was like reading a book. Each note correlated to a key on the piano. There was no substance behind this.

My teacher sang opera. She was handicapped from polio, had huge braces on her legs and only got around by heaving her legs around her and using crutches. When I played the piano, she hummed along. I think she compensated for her handicap by being extraordinarily gifted and developing it. Her voice was so melodic; I became intimidated to count out loud. I didn't want to sing the beats, so I handicapped myself through my own fear. Not recognizing this, my teacher continued to sing out the counts.

A whole note is an open circled symbol that has no stem on it. It means to hold it out for the entire count assigned to a measure. If beats were counted out in groups of four, then it was a four beat measure. A whole note would resonate for that long. So, in my piano world my teacher would sing out rapidly one two three fooooooouuuurrr until she felt the full measure had been acknowledged.

Consequently, I gained an appreciation of music, but not the theory behind it. She made it beautiful. If I had an aptitude for music, perhaps it would not have mattered about counting out loud: I would have been more confident.

Throughout the years I should have comprehended the chords behind the music, the keys, major or minor. At some point it would have clicked.

165

Instead, four flats were four flats: I didn't know what key they represented. Sharps were symbols that meant go one half step up from the original note.

A musically inclined person would make the connection and after six years of piano instruction would more than likely be able to play with or without music, read a sheet with simply chords written on it, change keys midstream, (that means going up or down so many steps in pitch), or memorize music. I had none of that.

Yet I felt I played fluently and brilliantly. I could do justice to all the classics, accompany any singer or choir in perfect rhythm stroked out by the conductor, and appear as a prodigy to those who knew nothing about music.

When I was 14 years old my piano teacher told me a story about a student she felt played mechanically and sloppily. She said she reported this back to the student's mother and received an irate response denying they could be talking about the same person. The confrontation had disturbed my teacher, due to the extent of the Mother's denial.

In a matter of months after that conversation, my teacher fired me. She said that she had taught me as much as she possibly could and that we had reached my pinnacle. Never did she say an unkind word to me; only gracing me with her beautiful smile and encouragement to follow my passion whatever it was.

Looking back, I realize that Mother in her tale was mine and the student was me. I really was not the prodigy. Not because I couldn't be, but because my heart was not in it. Music should be one's passion.

Perhaps I disproved my point and contradicted myself, but I don't think so. Some people only have an "ear" for music and cannot read a note. Many times it is because they have not had formal training; primarily because they coped without it. Additionally, their ear is so good they can play anything they hear; which to this day remains a mystery to me. The people I know who are gifted with this talent generally are not interested in reading music until much later in life.

By the time someone reaches that spot, learning is not so appetizing, due to how basic music theory is.

I already described measures, but if you really want to yawn, try to learn what a treble clef and bass clef symbol stand for. A treble clef represents the

notes you play with your right hand. Bass clef
symbols represent the left hand notes. The notes are
written across five lines crossing a paper, which is a
staff. Maybe some of you had the childhood music
teacher who had an implement holding 5 pieces of
chalk that would trace the lines across the chalkboard
with one swipe of the hand.

Math helps to understand counting beats in a
measure. Notes are divided into fractions such as
quarters, eighths, sixteenths, and on. When there are
4 beats in a measure, then 4 sixteenth notes equal 1
beat. A logical adult mind might say, but how?
That's ¼ so wouldn't it be ¼ of a beat? Nope!

In my estimation, it is simpler to teach a child,
because children don't question these principles; they
just accept it as fact and proceed without question.

Music can be a form of healing. The musician
is the healer and their instrument is the vehicle.
There are many types of music therapies out there.
One type of therapy is used to strengthen the core
muscles because our core muscles tighten as we listen
to music.

We insomniacs use music. We'll talk more
about this in chapter 31.

To sum it up, music can be taught through appreciation (passion for music) or by taking the trained ear and correlating the melodies to symbols. This is only my subjective observation; something for you to chew on as you push toward slumber.

Hmmm, chewing, chew, food, cake, pizza, diet!

Chapter 24: Dieting

Just the word diet makes me gain weight. Many of my friends agree: when we consider depriving ourselves, we begin to desire what we cannot have. My stomach is literally growling while I write this and I just ate.

Talk television offers more varieties of diets than a greenhouse has blooms. It is beyond confusing and gives one far too much to think about when we hear about all the pitfalls of wheat, gluten, sugar, sugar substitutes, processed food, red meats, laboratory produced vegetables, fast food, trans-fats, vitamin intake, filtered water, antibiotic injected chickens, mercury laden fish, preservatives, sodium, whole grain versus pretend whole grain bread, white rice versus brown rice, red slime, etc. Then there are the arguments about caffeine and alcohol intake: some studies say coffee has health benefits and other studies claim the risks outweigh the benefits: the same with alcohol. Where in the world does one begin?

I think the one that gets me the most is the controversy of what constitutes a proper amount of daily vitamins. Many say that we can't get it all from food, no matter how organic we go. The term "expensive pee" and my doctor's, "you'll just poop it out", (gross), circle around. Then I heard a doctor on television news today claiming that we must have vitamins to "grease our wheels." Add to that the knowledge that some vitamins are stored in the liver and the worries begin all over again.

Fad diets don't attract me. So many times I have had acquaintances enthusiastically begin the regimen prescribed and they quickly lose weight. The problem with this is that they seem to gain it back just as rapidly once the diet is completed. The talking heads may say it is because their metabolism slowed down while it was being deprived. I couldn't eat only protein, only carbs, no fruit, or do a purge. Mind you, I'm not knocking those of you who can do the purge where you try to cleanse your colon and flush toxins. I just happen to be a person who eats every 2-3 hours in small proportions and doesn't do well without food.

Some of you may have taken the *supplements* that are supposed to speed up your metabolism, thus burning calories at a higher rate. Worse, you use the supplements only to have the FDA remove them from the market as unsafe.

On the other side of the diet coin are the dieters who do not change what they consume, but do step up the workouts: almost to the point of fanaticism. The difficulties begin when the dieter cannot keep up with the routine they created for themselves, because it is hard to maintain such a pressing schedule. I always feel terrible for those who persevere only to experience an injury, calling a halt to all their workouts. Getting back into the swing of things after they heal can be a challenge.

Dieting is psychological. My entire life I have worked out, faithfully. It is not optional: I make it part of my life; my natural high. There are days when I can barely face the treadmill, but I wearily climb on. My battle begins when I think I can justify more calories because I did 30 minutes of cardiovascular exercise. However, realistically, the calories I add do not offset the calories I burned.

I do believe the trainers who say that you burn calories at a higher rate for several hours after a workout compared to those who do not work out. For me, I must be entertained when I work out. I like exercising at home or outdoors, so I either have music or a television on to distract me from what I'm putting my body through. To contradict myself, I will not have music while I'm outdoors. I allow myself to get lost in my thoughts. I try to do things I enjoy. When I exercise outdoors whether it is aerobic yard work, a fast-paced walk, jogging or tennis, I make sure I am aware of my surrounds and take in what inspires me. For me dieting is a word I replace with lifestyle. I make choices that I'm passionate about and that are realistic for me.

The First Lady changed our food pyramid to a plate. Our Nation's school children can now visually see what their plates should look like. A visual helps me tremendously. I find myself subconsciously comparing my plate to the healthy prescribed one.

I maintained my weight once I gave up the idea of a diet. I decided to stick to the tried and true: move more eat less, but in moderation and never to the extreme. I have found this works in all aspects of life: moderation!

Am I egotistical enough to think that is it, the secret to everyone's success? No way no how! Everyone is different and struggles in their unique way. We are all driven by different things and run to the beat of our own drum.

So when I am at a restaurant and they say "white rice or brown", I still waffle. I become conflicted between what I like in contrast to what is better for me. I think about the "fist" a nutritionist will hold up while declaring our stomach is no bigger than our fist, so neither should our combined portions be.

When I listen to fitness experts they will say that their clients don't eat *enough* calories while dieting I am fascinated by the looks of surprise they have on their faces. They get to eat more? Cool! Their metabolisms will actually slowdown in an effort to preserve fat. Then there are the myths that fat replaces muscle and muscle replaces fat yet I heard an expert say that fat and muscle are two different things and not interchangeable. What is a person to believe?

Doctors encourage their patients to eat more fiber; use whole grains, and keep their bowels moving at least twice a day. (A.W. did this from my old office.) They'll ask you, "What color and texture are your stools? Are they heavy or light? Do they have blood in them? I turn red even right now as I do not like to speak about feces as you already know.

Flip on the television and you'll hear doctor say that wheat makes you gain weight. Hold on there: I thought wheat was fiber and fiber moved waste through your body. Isn't a body sans waste lighter than one that is impacted with it? What in the world is a consumer supposed to do?

I can tell you what they're not to do! Do not as a thin person tell your overweight friend that you gained 3 pounds and are unable to lose it. They'll want to bitch slap you. Don't puff out your tiny little stomach and state "Oh I'm sooooo full: why did I eat so much?"

In the end, I listen to my own body. I use common sense, ignore the fluff, assess whether or not the presenter of miracle diets has something to gain besides weight, and filter the information. Bedtime is a great time to filter. I use the quiet to digest not my food, but information overload I've been subjected to throughout the day.

Sometimes when I'm overloaded I dream totally irrational dreams, like when my bright little goddaughter appeared unexpectedly in my dreams.

Chapter 25. Mollee

I see my goddaughter, Mollee, in my dream. Yes, I managed to fall asleep for a few blissful moments. Mollee is at a busy intersection in Tucson. It is a very wide intersection, 3 lanes in each direction where cars are traveling 35-45 MPH.

Now Mollee is a cherished child: her parents never even let her go to sleep at night without being tucked in by them. They make sure all their dates end at 8pm (yes, some people can find things to do in the early evening), and then they do their bedtime ritual with her; read stories, brush teeth, brush hair; you get the idea.

Dreams being what they are tend to be in character, yet strangely off kilter, as is this one.

As Mollee's parents sit in lawn chairs in the McDonald's parking lot on the SW corner of this intersection they proudly watch Mollee march toward the crosswalk.

She depresses the crosswalk signal and as the light changes, she bends her elbows at her sides with her hands pressed upward and out, halting traffic as she confidently steps into the busy intersection and begins to cross 6 lanes to the opposite corner.

I found myself observing all of this in my dream, catching my breath, gasping when a car makes a right turn on red directly toward her little outstretched arms. Narrowly, the car misses her.

Somehow, Mollee makes it to the opposite side, only to repeat the process all over again, this time traversing from the SE corner to the NE corner. Again, I think? The same set of circumstances repeat themselves as Mollee continues with outstretched hands to weave her way through the traffic.

This process continues: NE corner to NW. I'm still in a state of shock: what is wrong with her parents? Why are they lounging in their chairs, arms crossed in front of their chests, proud smiles on their faces?

"What are you doing?" I ask them. "My parents didn't allow me to cross the street until I was 10, and that was a quiet neighborhood street that had a 4-way stop on the corner: go help her!"

At that point, Mollee is making her last lap: NW corner to SW corner. Her mom tells me that it's all part of her enhancement, a rite of passage: 5 year olds are much more mature than they were in my era. (Here's where the wandering mind comes in: a dream tangent). Era, what do they mean Era? What am I; a relic? I'm not that old, for goodness sake! I wasn't exactly born yesterday, but I do remember yesterday.

I wasn't even allowed to ride my bike to school until I was 10, either, and I had to get a bike license for that from a test on the school playground. I was very proud of the license sticker that was adhered to my bike: it represented my great bike riding skills: I could weave in and out of the orange cones, all the while demonstrating my hand signals. Walking? I would walk 7 blocks to school with a cello, in the ice and snow, and still I hadn't earned the right to cross my street. (I know; wah wah wah!) Wait a minute; didn't I have to cross the street when I walked to and from my elementary school? Wasn't I a cross guard? Oh yeah, that was when I was in 5th and 6th grade, so I had reached aged 10.

My cello, by the way, had a hole in the canvas case that zipped around its bulky form. It was one of those instruments rented from the school. Kids would see me trudge by with it, twice a week, (orchestra days), and they decided to name it my air conditioned cello.

If that wasn't embarrassing enough, housed inside the air conditioned case was a bright painted red 6"x 9" wood block, a 2 foot piece of looped rope glued to it, with a ¼" hole drilled in the middle of the block. This was for that peg that pulls out of the cello's bottom to hold it in place while straddling the cello. The blocks' string looped onto the leg of a folding chair. The cello peg would pop into the drilled block hole: between the rope captured by the chair and the peg in the hole, my cello would not slide out from my grasp.

Ah those were the days….the days, oh Era, oh no, there's a car heading toward Mollee with her outcast hands. I gasp and wake up!

Dang-it, I'm awake again. Now, what can I do to settle my rapidly beating heart, my illogical anger at Mollee's parents, and the fact I'm no longer asleep?! I let my mind go once again.

Chapter 26: Misinterpretation

I stayed at my sister's home recently and told her about this weird dream I had. It was very obscure. In my dream I had a pillow and I was throttling it: just shaking the snot out of it. I would fluff it up then punch it down: the pillow had a mind of its own and I thoroughly resented that it would not conform to my machinations.

My sister upon hearing this immediately pounced on my dream remembrance and said "that means you're irritated with me: I believe dreams and you're mad; I know it!"

Well, first of all, I'm an adult woman and I no longer get mad at my sister. I am not pulling your leg! I haven't been pissed off at her in a very long time. I was a guest at her house, and although bossy, I was secretly pleased at her big sister act: conversely it made me feel loved since we both were deprived in our teen years of a Mother.

However, after her dream interpretation I was getting there rapidly. Now I WAS annoyed! Maybe I could have used the pillow as a metaphoric replacement for my bossy sister! Or maybe she had not considered that she was annoyed with me and I was the pillow: she was the aggressor. I became confused.

"Why are you saying this?" I demanded! Are you saying you're the pillow or am I? Because if you're the pillow, I know damned well you won't be a feather pillow because it would make too much of a mess and you're a neat freak!" (Imagine if someone was eavesdropping on our conversation at that moment: they would have been hitting their ears with the palm of their hand as if to say *I'd better adjust my hearing because that makes no sense!)*

Whoops! I may have gone too far. Yep, the gleam in my sisters' eyes confirmed it as she cockily reminded me that I could not be the feather pillow because I was allergic to feathers!

I reacted with, "Well who said they were feather pillows, anyway? It's not like I saw feathers floating around the room or anything".

This was becoming far too big of a deal. I was positive that all my mind had been sorting out that night was the ability to mold those pillows into the perfect shape for my head and neck and when they didn't comply, I shook them into submission. Plain and simple! Why make it so complicated?

Bored To Sleep

Some people have dreams that change their lives. They feel transported to another place and time, where time doesn't appear to be important. They just are: no drama, no arguments or pain but their very own utopia.

Others feel they are psychic: the kind of dream that appears to come as a warning or a vision perhaps. It feels so real and upon awakening the dreams remain; thick, intense, and worrisome. These are the reflective dreams requiring much contemplating.

I'll give you an example. The week before 9/11/01 happened, I was in England. When I went to sleep I felt a surge as if a vacuum was sucking my soul right out of my chest and I was out in the sky witnessing a bizarre scene. Floating from earth to sky like paper dolls connected together, service men and women in World War II khaki colored garb were joined by hands stiffly at sides, staggered, one high, one low, still holding hands. Men were in short sleeved shirts and long pants; women were in the uniformed dresses. They were floating skyward in the chain design. There was a huge fist filling the sky larger than any cloud previously seen. It was clasped with the index finger pointing up. It was a masculine hand. The members connected to each other were in a trance like state, appearing more as zombie like vapors floating to the hand rather than cognizant human beings.

I felt my breath suck back into my chest, and looked around in my own bed: the image indelibly stamped on my mind. The first thing I wanted was an interpretation; not a misinterpretation. At first I thought they were World War II men and women who had perished and in my dream I was watching their souls drift away. Now I think it was a warning but who would have believed a military spouse living in England. And it's open to interpretation. First I'd have to believe in visions and second, I wouldn't have even thought of that interpretation except that 9/11/2001 happened just days after the dream: soul after soul floating away to the sky. I wondered.

I'm sure we've all had those dreams and try to connect the dots to something real. You may get that eerie feeling and hope that it's just a coincidence. I did the same thing about my daughter. I dreamed she had tubes sticking out from her abdomen and that she was in a hospital room and I couldn't get to her. The very next month she ended up having emergency abdominal surgery in a hospital. She had tubes draining the fluid from her belly, post-surgery. Was it maybe a Mother's intuition? Who knows? But what I do know is we all dream when we're lucky enough to fall asleep and they aren't always as deep as the ones that feel like premonitions.

Chapter 27. Pink Elephant and Pancakes

I was at a church: a large church; probably 700-800 people at any given time. The worship center was divided into three adjoining rooms. Spoking off these rooms were other smaller classroom size areas.

The first room was arranged in a semi-circular fashion, pews curving around in the half moon shape, facing a center raised stage and podium. It was the sanctuary. The minister could stand and deliver his sermon while the podium held his text. His wireless microphone allowed him to wander from side to side, gesturing with exaggerated hand movements to underscore his point.

In the room just off to the right of the main sanctuary was a music room where the worship band led the congregants in a rousing thirty minutes of worship. The drums pulsated, while the bass guitar hummed its vibrating electrical pulses accompanied by a keyboard capable of emulating an entire orchestra. As the music throbbed, the crowd became caught up in the worship, music, words, and sense of community.

To the rear of this music room was a practice room. It was setup in stadium style seating, rows of bleachers once again in the semi-circular pattern, facing a performance stage. The stage had a grand piano, 2 guitars, practice drums, keyboard, saxophone and a trumpet. Off to the side was an orchestra pit: room for one each; violin, viola, cello, and upright bass.

Fronting the instruments there was plenty of room for the singers to perform, along with actors.

The stage was elevated 3 feet: below it at ground level there was room for a nativity scene: the aisles wide enough between the bleachers to parade camels, sheep, or in this case, an elephant!

On this particular Sunday morning the church building was alive with the sounds of church-goers and the participants were eagerly engaged in the mornings' activities.

Since there were so many patrons, the 3 rooms were used to stagger the schedules by cycling the worshipers from musical skit to worship music to sermon.

Bored To Sleep

I was late. This upset me because my habit is to be 10 minutes early for anything and everything. It removes the angst for being on time. This day was the exception and my anxiety was revved into high gear!

When I entered the church doors, the hum of activity had permeated the walls. I wonder which room I should start in. I opted for the musical skit and a seat in the bleachers. When I walked into the room and began to climb the bleachers, I noticed the room was vacant: "shoot", I thought, "I had missed it". From my peripheral I saw a large shadow and I froze in place. A large plaid pink elephant not quire full grown was walking between the rows of bleachers, swinging its trunk. A trumpeting sound filled the room but not from the brass section as I was fervently hoping at that moment!

The plaid monstrosity spied me and made a beeline straight for me. Somehow the bleachers had all become one level, totally within reach of the creature.

It was not a friendly sound coming from that mouth. The lips were peeled back and short white razor sharp teeth were bared and pointed in my direction. Frightened, I scanned the room for the nearest exit. I could see the doorway leading to the sermon room. The elephant was frighteningly psychic: it knew I want to get to that doorway. I tried to make a run for it but the elephant was right there to block me, baring its teeth once more. I was petrified and irrationally my stomach began to growl.

When I'm not thinking about being 10 minutes early, I'm thinking about when I'll eat again. The fact that I eat every 2-3 hours easily translated right into my dream. I imagined I smelled food in another doorway. It led neither to the worship or sermon rooms, but to a banqueting hall. I saw a buffet setup: there were finger foods, little meatballs speared with colorful toothpicks, and piles of buttermilk pancakes stacked in towers of a dozen, each. Maple syrup permeated the air.

I had two missions on my mind that melded into one: get out of the musical skit room and into that banquet! I tried to run zigzag between rows to confuse the elephant that was pursuing me in a grid like fashion. Just as I thought that plaid pink stuffed animal come to life is going to capture me and eat me for its main course before I even get to mine, a zookeeper calmly walked into the room and said, "Oh there you are, come here you!" Docilely the pink elephant complied, walking with him looking neither left nor right.

I made my escape. When I entered the banqueting hall, I saw that all the food was gone! I was absolutely deflated and my stomach is growled its protest. I decided to circle the buffet and there at the far side was the pot at the end of the rainbow: pancakes, golden luscious, fluffy, and stacked.

My plate was filled, syrup drizzled over the top and I dove in. Pure bliss! It was short lived, because the sermon room had dismissed and the rotation had begun. It appears no one was hungry, but everyone was interested to hear why I was absent. I tried to explain, but to no avail. Finally it occurred to me to roll up my pant legs, because there covering my legs was a pink plaid pattern! Validation: ah it felt oh so good!

Once I was awake and filtered that weird dream, I remembered that our dog Gertie once had a plaid pink elephant guaranteed to last for life. Gertie chewed the snot out of that elephant and would shake it back and forth in her huge jowls for all she was worth. I wondered; was that elephant getting revenge on me in my dreams? Isn't the subconscious great?

Chapter 28. Social Media Etiquette

Cyber-world: it has taken over our lives. Do any of you get sick of social media? I do! There are simply days many of us would like to disconnect. Who thought "unplugged" would migrate from music to communication? Why did I listen to Cyber-Granny, anyway? I wondered if she would have continued to embrace the newest technologies.

I'm sharing this with the assumption you are Facebook savvy, since it is among the first of the many ways to reach out, as well as the old My Space. I have interviewed many people about what they consider to be proper Facebook Etiquette. Here are the phrases I heard the most:

Facebook:

We don't honestly care what your political views are.

Don't use your personal Facebook to promote your business if that's all you post about. If you insist, do it occasionally and then create a "page" for your business, pay for it and get on with it.

If your posts are all slanted to the same thing time and again, we're bored with you. When we're bored with you we turn off your notifications and remove you from our newsfeed: we do not "unfriend" you, however. Our "friends" suffer hurt feelings when they are "unfriended". Heaven forbid we would offend anyone.

If you do not like a post, then type in "unlike" under comments since there is not an unlike button.

Be confrontational only if you are wishing to push buttons that could start a long diatribe from other members.

Lock down your settings if you don't want friends of friends or the public to view your posts: otherwise, expect to see comments you may not like from people who do not know you. Etiquette does not require always being friendly to people unknown to you.

If you post pictures out there, label them would you? Unless you post these to a specific group who know what in the heck you're talking about, then label them! My groups of peeps say there is nothing more annoying than seeing pictures of people that they don't know. If it is a casual friend but you still want to comment, what is there to say? "Nice pic of I don't know?"

When labeling, make sure you don't just write under the person's name: "Becky". Say, "Becky, my cousin". Now it all makes sense. I guess I'm sounding like Miss Manners, aren't I?

We don't want to see your sexy profile picture unless you're specifically using the media for dating purposes. If you're married, put the girls away.

Instagram:

Instagram is a form of social media that allows users to instantly post square pictures out to cyber-world. For you techies, I apologize for the simplicity of that statement.

If you want to post specific photos of yourself, then use a hash tag to promote it to the right audience. Example: If it is a "who's the prettiest girl on the cheerleading squad" picture, then hash tag it: #prettycheerleader

Hash tags are used to group Instagrams and Twitter to target a specified audience: use them!

Twitter

This is not a judgment on my part; simply feedback I have received.

Quite a few consumers of Facebook do not wish to see all your "tweets" included on your Facebook statuses: they do not care you are at Starbucks with your aunt Emma. If they did, then they would follow you on Twitter.

Just like Instagram: Twitter allows you to group your tweets by hash tag: know your audience!

Don't be consistently hateful: (think certain Hollywood actor's public persona).

If all your tweets are self-promotion, then we're going to ignore you. We are put off.

Your tweets go out into Cyber-world forever. You cannot retrieve them! Use that as motivation before you hit "post". The most innocent of people have had their posts misinterpreted unjustly. If your friends take a questionable picture of you, make them swear they won't post it on Twitter.

Snap Chat Pictures

By the time you read this, some of these will be old school and there were will be a lot more not on the list. But, I really like this one. My son introduced me to it when he was riding in the car with us and kept holding his phone and laughing. Every once in a while a photo would quickly appear and then just as quickly disappear. What was it? Someone texted him a photo that can appear for a specified time frame; as short as 1 second. The pictures delete automatically after that period is up. They say a picture is worth 1000 words and this new way of chatting seems to accomplish just that. But nothing is for certain and it is said there have already been software programs written that will retrieve your unretrievables.

I say we snap a shot of ourselves yawning, reading this book: that would be great for publicity!

Linked-In and other Networking Sites

The number one etiquette breech I hear about Linked-In is that sometimes people forget it is to network with professional contacts. Remember it is designed for your career: we do not want to see your neighbors' cute puppy! We want to see you!

Blogs

Not as many people are as vocal about blog etiquette. To them, this is someone's personal journal. If you don't want to read their innermost thoughts, then don't log into it. Unlike Facebook, you only see that one person's commentary unless someone has posted in the "comments" section which many bloggers pre-approve.

Being preachy or judgmental about what a person blogs just does not seem to be appropriate.

You-Tube

You know, I don't have a lot to say about You-Tube. It is one of those sites people have not complained about as much to me.

What you post out there you intend to share with everyone for whatever motivation you have. Remember, others out there may not see it through your eyes and judge you for it. Maybe your motivation is to post something that is so unbelievably funny that Hollywood will pick it up. Good luck: the odds are not very high. Make sure it is worth it in the scheme of things. It is a huge source of amusement for many: especially the animal videos.

Text Messages

Annoyance #1, hands down: why are you texting me paragraphs? Wouldn't it be easier to call?

What happened to "reach out and touch?" an old telephone commercial.

If it's brief; text. If it requires a lengthy conversation, then please dial the $%(_) phone!

Sometimes we want to hear your voice: it makes us feel special.

Use texts for brevity in conversation; not to replace the spoken language!

Watch for auto-correct. Some of the word replacements although quite funny, just might make late night television fodder.

Cautionary Tale

Social media touches many parts of our lives. We even use it in the workplace to a limited extent via instant messaging throughout the offices.

In summary, my pilot group gives one last word of caution. If you put it out there, as mentioned above, you cannot take it back. (Think computer forensics).

Future employers will use the social media to learn about prospective candidates. Be wary! You may think that they only "google" you after your interview, but in reality, they desire to see what you're about before you sit before them in the interview chair.

Employers feel they have an advantage when they are armed with what you are like outside the workplace. Fair or not, keep that in the back of your mind. Any blog you comment on could be public property for all eyes to see. They will look you up, so be careful which picture pops up. True story: we hired a handyman and he gave us a link to his website. When we googled him, guess what came up: A picture of him drunk and dancing while half dressed.

Yawn! I'm even bored with this topic now! Let's move on to things we write: our isms as I like to call them.

Chapter 29. Isms

Fondly referred to in my family as KC-isms, I throw out phrases I have either heard all my life or made up myself: After all, someone needs to start the trend, right? You have probably already seen me reference them in previous chapters.

We all use them; some of us more than others. Some of you may use them unintentionally while others make a point to. Recently, I had a piece of information shared in confidence with my oldest daughter and she repeated it to all her siblings. Why you ask? Because I used a phrase she did not understand, so it did not even register. I said, "This is between you, me and the fencepost." When I confronted her about this and stated, "But I told you not to share it", she was perplexed. I repeated the phrase and she looked blankly at me.

So to make my point, I used social media and put the phrase out there: "Hey everyone: what does "between you, me and the fencepost" mean?" Depending on the age group, I got "I don't know" to the real meaning. I ended up proving the point to both of us.

So, what DOES it mean? Here's where it gets sticky: (sticky, another ism?) Different people have different interpretations. For the purpose of this chapter, I am not going to give you the official internet interpretation; I am going to provide the KC definition. So here we go!

Ism: "This is between you, me and the fence post". To me that means you and I are out maybe in a pasture, a blade of grass between our teeth, one booted foot up on the lowest rung of the fence, arms leaning against the post. We are casually "shooting the breeze". (I'll come back to that one in a minute). There is no one to hear the confidences we exchange except that fence post: an inanimate object not capable of repeating my words. Need I say more?

"Shooting the Breeze". Are we really shooting into the air, hoping to hit something substantial and thereby prove air has mass? No, it is not scientific, it just is a colorful way of saying we're casually speaking. What does it mean? I don't know: but I do know the context in which to use it. Maybe it means, spewing our words out into the air, just for the purpose of dialogue and nothing more.

"Screwed up my Courage". This one really caused controversy. In my book "The Corn Stalker:

An Uncomfortable Truth", I opened with this. Due to the discussion, I ended up editing it out. I had a friend call me with a panicked tone to her voice. "You opened your book with an error!" Since I've probably read and edited that book easily 100 times, I cited, "It took 38 years to *screw up the courage* to look a killer in the eyes." I repeated this to her and she was perplexed. "Yes, yes, that's it: that is an error"! Offended, I began to explain that no it was quite accurate and exactly as my character would have talked. This is one ism I had to look up, because my friend, the intelligent being she is, was adamant I was incorrect.

When I explained this ism to her, it was not according to the historical definition. I said, "when you take a screw and begin turning it with a screwdriver into the wall, after a short time, it begins to make progress and chew its way through the point of entry: in the same manner, my courage is the screw and as I work it into its intended target, it becomes stronger." Made sense to me while said friend was still perplexed.

I tried again, this time with an official explanation. I stated, "It is an old Scottish term demonstrating ones desire to *work-up* their courage."

Her response was (as I heard her computer keyboard clicking away, still unconvinced :) "Oh, well I'll be, it does exist."

Anxious to get one last dig in she said, "But no one is going to understand it: I didn't know, and I asked others, too". What would you say to someone who didn't get your ism?

So I said what any defensive author would say. "Then consider yourself educated, and maybe since it's in my book, it will be resurrected!'

I used her "I'll be" just now and realized that, too, is an ism. It would be defined as "knock me over with a feather". Ism to Ism: isn't that something?

I've been "trying like the devil" to make my point to you and to of course, bore you to sleep. *Trying like the devil* by my understanding is that the devil is relentless so he doesn't give up: neither do I.

The subject of the devil may put you in "the pits" or you may say "it's the pits!" Maybe it's clearer if I say "I couldn't get any lower and the lowest place I can think of is the pit of hell." Point made!

While we're on religious statements, how about this one? "I had to rob Peter to pay Paul". My kids think this one is ridiculous: they think it has no meaning at all. "Ah, but it does!" I say. Peter and Paul were followers of Jesus: they were poor, giving up their means to follow him. They did not have money, so if Peter needed money and asked Paul for it, it would be for naught (nothing). It means I can't get help from there, because there IS no help there!

"The proof is in the pudding". I'm confused about this one: I really don't know. Let's surmise. Maybe the pudding is chocolate, rich and creamy. You dip your spoon into the bowl, lift the lusciousness up to your mouth, roll it around and have a taste experience. It is good; why? Because the pudding proved it. My best guess is that many of you are reading this and saying "That's not it: that's not it". Maybe it's because if prepared properly, the pudding is firm yet creamy. (Seriously, again, get your mind out of the gutter!) The proof is when you see it.

Ever have an adult give you an ism that is supposed to say it all and comes without explanation? Here is one that irritates me to this day! "If wishes were wagons, we'd all take a ride". I've also seen it as "If wishes were horses, beggars would ride". This was recited whenever I wanted something that was not forthcoming. It took me years to roll this one over in my mind and I still didn't get it. I have deliberated and decided that it must mean, we all want things, and because we do, we'd all get into the wagon of life and go for a roll. But, we don't all have wagons and we all cannot go for a ride. I'm still confused.

What if we did go on that ride and it was on a steep incline in the downward direction? And, what if you had someone pushing you off as you screamed at push off and then they had the nerve to yell, "Don't get your panties in a bunch!" First interpretation? Rude! Second? You must be uncomfortable but get over it, it's just a wedgey and you can always pull it out of your butt! Yes, I see that pulling out if of your butt is another ism. Apparently I cannot speak without them. It's "six to one: ½ dozen to the other" that I'll use them: two ways of saying the same thing. (I hate that one, too, by the way, because it requires me to think.) I'm always asking my husband: "six to what, or a dozen to what?"

In conclusion, isms underscore a phrase: much like swearing. They highlight a fact, add pizazz to a statement, and allegorically paint a picture for the recipient. Isms are good!

Bored To Sleep

What is not good is what I recently experienced at a local park.

Chapter 30: Dumpster Diving

Our community has large trash pickup day twice a year: one in the Fall and one in the Spring. During this time, we are allowed to put large items out such as mattresses, furniture, large yard debris, and anything not toxic to the environment. It is a time of great interest for pickers: people who cruise neighborhoods for used items they can later use for resale or personal use. These are the same people who frequent yard sales looking for a find, often returning at the conclusion of the yard sale to make a lump sum purchase for their remaining items; knowing full well they'll go to Good Will or the Salvation Army as a donation if they don't ask for the items.

Trucks literally drive up and down the neighborhood over and over waiting for these treasures that they can reclaim. There is a popular TV show called "The Pickers", so interest is even higher than before. Pickers make money: they can use the internet, swap meets, or their own yard sales to advertise.

You would not believe how quickly items are snatched up. Even though we're not allowed to put computer monitors, paint, and things like car batteries out, we all do it. It is with the knowledge that those items will not be there in the morning when the City trash collectors arrive. Our neighbor literally put their battery out on the curbside and within 60 seconds, it was gone; just like that. Everyone likes a bargain and everyone likes clearing out their garages, cupboards, basements, closets; anywhere they collect junk. It is a collective feeling of goodwill. We all get something out of it: either a more organized house or a real find. They say one man's trash is another man's treasure.

Once all the excess in my house is cleaned out, then it's time to hit those boxes that my husband has been saving, just in case he needed to return that new computer monitor, or return the receiver for his satellite dish. "Just in case we need it" is his motto. Mine is: "if you haven't used it in a year, then you don't need it." Since it is large trash pickup and we are fresh from watching "The Hoarders", my husband is mentally prepared to let go. Recycling is not included in this pick up, and I do not want to mix my recyclables in with the trash. The old boxes get to go in the next round.

Proud to do my civic duty, I flattened a bunch of excess boxes we had acquired that would not fit into our assigned recycling bin. A couple miles down the road, there was a local park that had big community recycling bins. I thought that I would combine taking my extra boxes with a trip to the park where I could then do laps around the walking trail. Two for one: I didn't waste gas and I did my part to lessen my environmental footprint. The sun was just rising and I knew the trail wouldn't be clogged with joggers at the crack of dawn. An added benefit was that it would still be relatively cool.

I carefully drove up to the park. The dumpsters there are fenced off in their own special area. Care must be taken to park several yards away from the dumpsters because of glass chards on the parking lot.

The bins were painted royal blue with portholes lined up along the sides, above shoulder height, I might add. It is difficult to cram boxes into these holes, which are about 18" in diameter, and the only other option is to heave these heavy lids up, which are hinged every 3 feet or so. Each bin must be at least 16 feet long and 6 feet high.

Bored To Sleep

The bins are placarded indicating this one is for glass, this one for paper, and the furthest one for cardboard.

On this trip I only had cardboard: some of the boxes were quite large and wouldn't cram into the 18" holes. With dread, I realized I needed to heave up a 3 foot lid while standing on my tippy toes and balance the box between my stomach and the hard metal of the bin. I struggled with the lid, got it up just enough to hold with my left hand while my right sought the box and tossed it in. I was going to have my work out before I even got to my jogging.

I repeated this motion several times; glad I was alone, not wishing to be a spectacle as I repeated my steps. Finally I got to the smaller boxes and began stuffing them through the holes. As I found certain sections full, I began moving down the bin towards the right. I heard a rustling. I decided to ignore it, but was secretly wondering if there were lizards or worse; rats living in the dumpster. I was terrified of crawling things that might startle me. With my arms full of small boxes, I looked up and saw a head pop out of the right port hole. The head had very thin dirty scraggly long hair, an unkempt beard, and blood shot eyes that were staring at me

208

while exhibiting a wide grin devoid of a few front teeth.

"Heeelllo! There's plenty of room down here!" In my surprise, I dropped a few boxes. I scrambled to pick them up, all the while keeping my eyes glued to his face, assessing if I was in danger. I decided to be nice: poor guy was sleeping inside a stinky bin full of cardboard and worse. So cheerfully I attempted to match his attitude with a sunny disposition while I said "thank you" and tossed the cardboard into him. He caught it and withdrew his head from the porthole.

"Have a nice day!" he said. At that point my heart was hammering harder than if I had just jogged 3 miles all the while my head was saying, "if only I had money on me, I'd give him some for food." I left feeling bewildered. I hit the side of my head, wondering if I had just hallucinated.

I comforted myself with the fact that maybe he was just dumpster diving, looking for hidden treasure as the pickers do, but in my heart I knew that was not so. He was in the recycling bin after all, and unless he was preparing to build a cardboard house, that was not likely. I prayed for his comfort and some small pleasures in his life: pleasures such as music.

Bored To Sleep

CHAPTER 31: The Effect of Music

Effect-Affect: both apply to music.

Do you ever turn music on in the bedroom to create a mood, say for sleep? You want to create an *effect* that will *affect* your desire for slumber.

In this scenario, possibly even as you are reading this, you may have music playing gently in the background. Perhaps something tranquil is being played such as a haunting cello; its bow slowly drawn across the strings in a mysterious sorrowful tune.

Maybe it is a violin, equally mysterious, but higher pitched. Or a piano: not haunting, but melodious: the ivories twinkling as the notes resonate gently through the speakers.

Some people prefer music as an accompaniment to sounds from nature; an ocean wave roaring into the beach while a piano imbues to make it complete.

I like no music at night; just the sounds of nature. For me the ocean is a little too strong in the context of sleep. I enjoy the gentle lapping of a lake, small waves slapping the pier in a rhythmic manner; constant and sweet.

Be careful not to be fooled. I purchased a CD with lake and nature sounds. I plumped up my pillows got my blankets just right and hit play. Ah bliss; the sounds of the miniature waves were doing their magic. I heard a bird here and there, a few crickets chirping and the far-off hoot of an owl. Every now and then there would be a roll of distant thunder.

Lulled into complete relaxation I was ready to fall asleep when suddenly. "Screech!! Screech!!!" I was jolted upright; because the producer of the CD thought it might be a good idea to include some hideous sounding tropical bird right into the mix. I am not kidding you: it sounded awful. This is the only place on the CD that has such a jarring sound. My cat thought it was so bad she began hitting the CD player with her paw, circling it round and round, looking for her prey. She did find the eject button, amusingly enough, which ended the torture for all of us.

I continued to listen to that CD, but always with my body tensing as I waited for that one bit to be over. Once it passed, I knew I could relax: the rest of the CD was glorious.

Since that time, I have not found the right balance for bedtime music, but my mom found it for mealtime. We had to listen to a Chicago radio program called "Candlelight and Silver: classical music for your dining pleasure." Every Thursday night this played while we ate in the dining room with glass dishes, forks on the left, spoons and knives on the right, napkins in our lap, while we learned about proper table manners. Unfortunately, the only lasting effect it had on me was to forever make an association between classical music and dinner time. Whenever I hear classical music, my stomach begins to rumble. It is rumbling even as I type this paragraph.

Music can affect our emotions. Yes, it triggers a response based on a memory; a connection from the physical to the psychological. How many times have we heard the crooner Barry White within the context of getting in the mood? His deep low voice caressing the words every woman wants to hear. Bliss! Maybe you prefer a little R&B to make you feel sexy, or a hard thumping back beat to underscore the moves you're about to put on your significant other, or *the cry in your beer music* a forlorn country song may elicit? They say misery loves sorrow!

Perhaps you've had a troubling event with equally sorrowful music in the background. Examples might be: Funerals, being stuck in the elevator with elevator tunes, music playing softly over speakers in a restaurant while you are being dumped, or maybe while receiving bad news of an emotional type and you had the radio on. In those circumstances, you may never wish to hear that music again, because it is a reminder of the time when…. We reminisce.

On a positive note, music can create a desired effect. I have a friend who is a well-known violinist. Once in a while someone will hire her to be at a pre-disclosed location with her violin in hand, dressed in formal attire, while they pop the question. It is a mood setter.

Sometimes mood setting isn't necessarily for a proposal but for filler. String quartets are commonly used to play during a formal function: a grand opening, or a celebratory party. While the patrons speak, mingle, and party, the music plays on. It is unobtrusive, discreet, and sets a tone with the party-goers who barely notice. The musicians are not upset: they do not expect it to be a hushed concert setting: they have a role and it is to give the people in attendance something sweet and warm to create an illusion of tranquility and maybe some class. You might think of it as sending a subliminal message.

Rock music is great for a good sweat breaking, adrenaline pumping workout. I like to run to the beat of the drum. I end up moving at a quicker pace without consciously being aware of it.

For those of you who like worship music, the Christian songwriter's melodies can be uplifting.

Last, many couples have a favorite song. It affects them deeply by stirring their emotions to a remembered point in time. It could be their first kiss, their first ah-hem, date, wedding ceremony, and on.

Music profoundly moves, inspires, and motivates us. When you are tired, try the music that enables you to empty your mind and simply savor the sweetness of it all! Or recite poetry!

Chapter 32: Simple Poems

Yes, we all have our childhood memories: poems recited to us in the classroom or at home. When I was little it was about a little lamb and red roses. Perhaps your audience sniggered as you stood up with trembling hands and shaky limbs to share your creation. Sharing your writing is extremely personal. It is something you and you alone crafted and you might be a little wary of the response others may give to your work.

We can use poems to make others laugh, cry, and even taunt. I am not going to recommend taunting because bullying is such a horrible pastime that too many kids participate in.

Tonight (assuming you attempt to sleep at night) we're going to play with funny poems. You do not have to be a poet laureate to create these. The whole idea is to have fun and make others laugh. Since these are so stupid, I do not care one iota if you laugh or groan, mock or demean my poems. They're only meant to be silly.

I'll do some below right off the top of my head and take the hit so that you can't possibly be more embarrassed than I am about to be. While making these up, I'll think of special occasions they could be used for. Feel free to borrow! I have no idea what I'm going to write, so hang tight, here we go.

Morning:

Oh morning you got here too early!
I need at least thirty more winks.
Without them I will be oh so surly.
A few more minutes to work-out the kinks!

Night:

Night time night time night time.
You said it would be the right time.
Yet it is never ever the good time.
For me to sleep on my own time.

A Birthday Wish (Have fun with these: it's a great opportunity to rub in someone's age)

Oh no, oh me, oh my, you are thirty?
Is that why at sports you are so slow?
Suddenly you can't stand to get your hands dirty?

Your spark is gone and you go with the flow?

Instead of French fries, you're chowin on
kale?
Rather than genuine draft beer it's now light
ale?
You forego the elevator and hike the stairs?
Worried you'll get love handles in pairs?
Stop fretting and enjoy the illusion
You're young, ya okay, that's delusion!

A Birthday Wish-Sentimental

Only you can make me feel sappy
The day of your birth makes me happy
The dawn of your day God smiled down
Without your presence I would drown.

Beauty of Nature

Oh nature you are so incredibly beautiful
I gaze on your wonder at the dawn of each
day
Preserving your splendor; we must be dutiful

The brilliance of your sunsets each shining

ray

Do not change the colors of the fish in the sea

Come on people let's do our part; let nature

be.

Dear John-Text version

I have ?4U

However @TEOTD

I thought it would be 4EAE

AAMOF

I am so 86 you

It's for ALCON

So B4N

You'll always be my BF

But for now BLNT!

(Interpretation or you won't appreciate the
artistry of that goodbye poem)

I have a question for you

However at the end of the day

I thought it would be for forever and ever

As a matter of fact

I am so over you
It's for all concerned
So bye for now
You'll always be my best friend
But for now better luck next time!

Dear John-Longhand

I have thought this thing through
We just don't click the way we used to
A future together I just can't see
Our relationship forward won't be
I will miss you and I did love you
But only as a friend: phew!

Valentine's Day-Love

How do I love you my cherished one?
A partner for life is what you are
If you left me I'd be done
I'll love you near or far.

Valentine's Day-humor

Bored To Sleep

Roses are red violets are blue

Our love together is true

You're into me I'm into you

I love you oh yes I do!

There are other ways to create poems: they don't always have to rhyme. Some poetry has prose or a rhythm to them: a bouncy poem. Here's some that don't rhyme.

Exercise if sweaty

Exercise is exhausting

Exercise is my Prozac

Exercise gives results

Exercise you are my friend

I am taken with you

Stunned by your beauty

Mesmerized by your smile

Haunted by your eyes

Captured in my soul

Be kind oh kindred spirit

You own my heart

I think I have given you something to think about. Maybe it'll inspire you to take your own risk, put yourself out there and share something goofy to make someone in your life smile.

For those of you who detest writing, this is a good way to show your humor. Hand written notes are sometimes the best thing when you've seen every greeting card imaginable and want to do something different. And best part, it's free!

Nevertheless, is anything in life ever free? Let's examine that next.

Chapter 33. For Free

You've heard the saying: "Nothing in life is free". (I'm finding it difficult to write this chapter because the one before has me wanting to do brief phrases and rhyme.) Let's take a deep breath and shake that one off.

With social media we are slammed with advertisements: on twitter self-promotionals: "click this link; read a copy of my book for free". When you click, you get to the site to download the e-book. On the page are other ads. Yes, the book is free, but if I'm the marketing director, then I am counting on you to gaze at the other ads.

On Facebook we want you to "like" our page. Sometimes after we do this, if our settings aren't locked down, then your status may read something like "Jane Doe liked KC Rhoads' Facebook page." And just for the record, I really do want you to look it up and "like" it. When you get there you may see that you can get one of my books for free on that certain date.

Facebook will also have "shares" that carry an image with a link "register to win or like to win a chance to win this free Ipad". Instagram may take a picture of something you can win for free. Pinterest is huge right now: you can have wish lists by pinning your coveted item to your board and then watch for it to become available when you can afford it.

Ideas can be for free. Pinterest has a myriad of ideas out there. Maybe it's an organizational idea or a quote: those are free. Want one of mine? "When you get kicked in the teeth don't bite back!" Inspiring, I know.

Recipes are free. People share these all over the internet. All have you to do is search on your favorite browser with the name of what you want to make, such as "stir-fry, meatloaf, cinnamon rolls, spiked punch, or chocolate chip cookies."

Television shows such as pop news shows will have a deal's day. Today with this promotional code you can get these products (which are being demonstrated on the television program) for 60% off with this promo code: XYZB4TODAY. When you get to their promo you might see something for free just for buying.

How about those infomercials on TV? This machine slices, dices, chews it up, spits it out, grinds, and purees. Why, it even feeds you. They go on to create several different food items all while a stopwatch is running in the background. "Look, you have a Panini sandwich with a carrot coleslaw and chocolate mousse for dessert and it only took 5 minutes to create: 5 minutes folks: now how you can pass this deal up? If you call the number now in the next 30 minutes, we'll throw in a spatula for free! This is a $10 value." A banner runs at the bottom of the page saying "only 352 left!"

How about relationships? A dating website may say something like "What will it cost you to meet someone?" You might respond with *well a lot, actually, like I might get stuck with the tab, have to buy flowers, hail a cab to get the heck out of there, or purchase a new outfit to impress the expected one.*

A relationship could also cause your heart to flutter. That's free. It could cause you emotional distress or it could give you a free boost to the ego.

You say; *but how is that really free: dating*? Dating can be free: it is the simple things in life, after all that many recall with the most nostalgia.

For free, you could:

- Visit a local museum
- Walk around the historical portion of a town center

- Go for a morning jog
- Walk in the snow: that'll make you feel alive with the cold stinging your cheeks!
- Find your local bike trail and pedal away. (unless you have to buy a bike first)
- Have an old movie night in front of the TV
- Popcorn and beverage in front of the fire with a library book
- Surf the internet
- Read your emails
- Write a letter: snail mail. It will only cost you a stamp but will make somebody happy
- Listen to your favorite music and dance
- In the summertime, go see the fireworks
- Attend music under the stars in your local park
- Peruse your town's website and see their free sponsored activities
- Attend church: (ours has free snack time in the middle of the service)
- Tennis at your local park or school

- Pick up the phone and call a friend: free but priceless
- Go through open houses and peek at how other people's homes look.
- Take your kids to the park and climb on the monkey bars with them
- Get free kids meals when you eat pizza on Tuesday nights
- Be a coupon user and buy one get one free

Are all of these things free? We're back to the original question. No they may not be. If you don't find a movie you like on TV you may be purchasing one over your cable company or running to your video box.

If you're jogging and twist your ankle, then you have to pay for a doctor's visit.

Listening to music under the stars may make you hungry, prompting you to buy something from the concession stand.

Your favorite dance music may be in the local bar and now a drink sounds really good to loosen you up.

Church may make you feel compelled to drop something into the offering plate even though visitors are usually told not to feel obligated.

Walking in the snow may require the purchase of a warm jacket.

Morning walks that are longer than a couple blocks may have you out purchasing good walking or running shoes.

You might not have a tennis racquet or may need to purchase balls.

The kids wear you out so badly at the park; you're in dire need of fast food.

Proud for writing a real letter, you realize not only are you out of stamps, but you don't have decent stationary. You find you really hate doing this and opt for a card instead: less space to fill up but more money.

You go to the open house and fall in love with the house. You decide you want to buy it!

You go to the open house and think their furniture looks better: you head to the nearest furniture store.

While walking, you notice the neighbor's yard looks better: it's the hydrangeas or the big maple tree in the front: you head to a garden center.

The museum is asking for a donation!

Your coupons say you must purchase two of said item before you get the third one free and to top it off, it's not even something you'd normally buy. Then you go down the promotional aisle while shopping for your coupon items and see something you just can't live without: an impulse purchase which the store is counting on!

In conclusion: maybe nothing's really for free, but in my opinion, the best things in life still are for free!

Chapter 34. Exhausted Thoughts

You are in bed and your mind is scattered. You actually don't to go to sleep because you need time to filter through the events of your day. What type of thoughts run through your head? If you could find a common theme, then maybe you could deal with them in advance.

What are some common topics that run around in our minds? Let's brainstorm.

Concerns:

Crap: I didn't work out. Should I reset my alarm to do it earlier?

Did I set my alarm?

The kid's lunches aren't made.

My homework isn't done: I need to get up early to complete it.

The house is dirty and I just have to get it cleaned.

The car needs an oil change.

I need to shave in the morning. (Men and women?)

What is for dinner tomorrow?

Should I take a lunch to work?

If only I had time to read more of that novel: what's coming next?

I need a vacation: where could I go?

What am I going to wear in the morning?

There's a meeting at work: I wonder what they want now?

Work: so much to get done: what should I do first?

Was that remark they said today meant as a barb?

I wonder who's on Facebook right now.

When am I getting paid and can I make it to payday?

I'm starving: maybe I should get up and eat something.

If I eat something then I'll feel guilty.

Does warm milk really make people tired?

People can be so rude.

Tomorrow's going to be so fun I want to plan my day now.

What was that song I heard in the car on the way home?

How long will it take me to get to that appointment tomorrow?

Bored To Sleep

When will that dog behind me stop barking?

Whose dog is it: The house to my right or the one directly in back? Wait, is that my ringtone?

These apartment walls are made of paper: they're doing it again?

I hear the rumbling of that bass when that car goes by every night: why always the same time? Don't they ever take a night off?

I don't want to attend that function tomorrow night: how do I get out of it?

My stomach hurts.

What time is it?

I'm in pain: make it stop!

You get the idea, right? We all have our own list in our heads. So, if it is a list, why not just write it down BEFORE retiring for the night? Here are some possible solutions. Obviously if I'm writing this, they didn't all work for me, but maybe it'll help you sleep?

As I mentioned in the prior paragraph, make a list:

List what I must do the next day.

List out what can wait.

Write down what is troubling me.

Prioritize my list.

If you're a writer, write down your ideas on a notebook situated on your nightstand, and then let the thought go. I come up with my best ideas at the most inopportune times.

Write down your dream if you managed to fall asleep at some point, so you can tell your friends how bizarre it was.

Make sure you're not starving when you go to bed.

Don't work out too close to bedtime: your endorphin rush could keep you awake.

Leave caffeine off your choice of beverages several hours prior to bedtime.

Don't drink too much alcohol before bed: I heard it can keep you awake.

Try a hot herbal drinks, perhaps, before turning in. It may allow you to relax your thoughts.

Avoid the computer or other mind stimulation before bed.

Have sex with your partner: if you're a man it'll knock you out, right?

Eat something with tryptophan; it makes you sleepy. Easy ones might be soy protein, frozen spinach (more palatable in a dip), turkey or other foul, game meat (yuck for me), seeds, warm milk, and many types of fish. I'm not an expert here, but this is what I've been told. Most of it sounds pretty disgusting to me, however.

Make your room dark.

If your utility budget allows; sleep in a cold room. (In the wintertime, no problem).

Turn your TV off if you have one in the bedroom.

If you like your TV on and drift to sleep, maybe you are fortunate enough to have a TV timer so it is set to go off in an hour.

I've heard Melatonin can make you tired; but for me it has the opposite effect and who knows if there are medical complications as research seems to change with the wind.

Give yourself time to meditate before bedtime and sort your thoughts out then: if something is troubling you, mind surf right then. Mind surfing is taking a thought and running it through to its logical conclusion.

After you mind surf, try to empty your thoughts while you meditate. If you're like me, you may not be so good about this. It reminds me of the movie, "Eat, Pray, Love" when Julia Roberts character tries this and finds it exasperating to erase her thoughts and relax.

Watch something mindless on TV before bed.

If something is bugging you, deal with it. Maybe it's as easy as sending an apology email to someone you didn't mean to jump all over that day.

If it's your relationship, resolve the issue if at all possible.

Think about solutions and write them down, then go to sleep.

Move nocturnal pets out of your room if they are jumping up and down on the bed, snuggling over your head or pushed up against you so that you're unable to move, much less get comfortable.

Pick up this book so you have something mundane to think about that has nothing whatsoever to do with anything that is most likely keeping you awake.

Don't go to sleep angry: you'll stew on it and in the morning it may take on proportions that are out of line with the real issue.

Relationships: they are complicated. I came up with my own relationship formula that it is my belief each couple should contemplate before they get too serious.

Chapter 35. The FFF

What you ask, are my triple F's: or treble F's if you're in the UK? You're thinking *anything with all those F's in it must be great for my relationship.*

Many counselors will advise young couples to deal with tough questions when they feel their relationship is going to be taken to a serious level.

The Triple F's are: Finances, Faith, and Frequency. Let me explain how I came up with these and how they may clear your mind of relationship difficulties, or at least give you a direction to take.

Finances:

Don't the experts mention money as being a bone of contention in relationships? Money problems can create a divide between couples. You may have one in the relationship who is a spend thrift. Spend thrifts can squeeze a dollar like no other. They have their priorities and could possess a cash only philosophy. When the allotted money runs out, then you wait for the next paycheck before you buy anything else. They pay their bills first.

To cope with a spendthrift it is helpful to have a wants versus needs frame of mind. Do you really need that new shirt if you already have 5 of that type and color hanging in your closet? Could you use coupons for your groceries and save money, or will you end up purchasing items at the grocery store you really don't need? If you're like me and love household items, especially for the kitchen, ask yourself if you need that stand mixer coupled with an expensive price tag, or if your baking habits are more suited to a portable hand mixer. You may find a $300 difference. Then you can justify to your partner that you saved $300 by not purchasing X, so maybe you can put it toward a big ticket item you both want.

You may love to shop and feel deprived when you haven't had a shopping expedition in a while. Shopping is therapeutic in your opinion, so you indulge yourself every so often. If you're coupled with a spend thrift, then it might be a good idea to communicate what each of you feel is important.

If you're not on a budget and can pretty much shop without having to determine the consequences, then this chapter really may bore you, which is all right, considering you are reading it in the first place!

Do you want to have kids someday, or already have them? Have you discussed if you'll have a college fund for your kids or is that a luxury you can't afford at the time? What about life insurance? Do you want to pay a monthly premium for it or sign up through your employer for additions to your employer-provided policy? Do you go nuts Christmas shopping? If on a budget, have you considered asking the family if they'll draw names instead, with a price limit for your gifting? Do you and your significant other agree on Christmas and whether or not to go all out?

What about birthdays? Do you each have expectations about what is realistic to give the other? Do you have to match the value of what they gave you? Don't assume you're of the same frame of mind if you haven't discussed finances yet.

Understand if you're both committed to the idea of having a savings account. I know we all hear we should have 3 months' salary set aside if single, and 6 months if jointly sharing expenses. In these days of recession, it is not so easy, but very handy if you get laid off. If you agree to save, then you must agree on how much of each check; say a percentage. If you belong to a church, then the question of tithing may arise, too.

Speaking of churches, which brings me to the next topic; Faith!

Faith:

You may not be a person who attends church at all, not believe in God, or find that you do better believing in God but don't want to go to church. Or, you could be a regular church goer who feels strongly about giving (tithing) a certain percentage of your income to your organization. (It could be a favorite charity, too). Many couples don't discuss faith before they get married. If you don't have kids, it may not even be an issue. But how many times do you hear of a conflict between couples after they have kids? One of you may want to take your kids to church, expose them to different religions, and have the desire to put them in Sunday school. You may believe this will set their moral compass and make them stronger individuals.

This is where it can get dicey: your partner may not think organized religion is appropriate for your child. If you haven't had this conversation it may become a huge bone of contention.

If you're both people of faith, but of divergent ones, then it may be necessary to have a meeting of the minds: a compromise or a choice. I have friends who married: one was Jewish and although he didn't embrace his religion, his parents did. Their desire was that their son would marry a good Jewish girl and that they and their future grandchildren would attend the local synagogue. He did not fall in love with a Jewish girl; he fell in love with a Protestant girl. They agreed ahead of time that if they had children, they would raise them as Protestant; and that they would both attend a Protestant church. It made life so much easier when the children did come into the picture. Prior to having children, neither practiced their faith, but when kids came into their lives, they decided it was time to practice what they had agreed upon in the beginning. They found a way to still acknowledge his Jewish heritage. Each year they have 2 banners included among their Christmas decorations: One says "Merry Christmas" while the other says "Happy Hanukkah". They have a Christmas tree and a Menorah: (a 9 branched candelabra; the 9th candle used to light the other 8.) When their kids get old enough, they are free to choose which faith, if any, they will practice.

Compromise again is key. The Jewish grandparents have had their wounded feelings salved by the fact our friends gave their son a Jewish first name.

If peace happens between a couple regarding faith and finances, then it is two less obstacles to get in the way of sex.

Frequency:

So often we hear about sex being a genuine issue within the framework of a relationship. Expectations are high between couples. When couples first meet, the infatuation is rampant, lust for one another is at the forefront of their thoughts and frequency may not be a divider at all. But, after a while have you found that although the flame still burns, it is more a smoldering ember than an all-out bonfire?

Couples sex lives can go awry when they assume their partner's sexual appetite matches their own. I know of people whose partner wants it every single night for the rest of their lives. Imagine their disappointment when a few years into the relationship their partner no longer finds it desirable to have sex daily? Their other half is disappointed, feels rejected, and sometimes undesirable. The vicious cycle begins: why can't we have sex, don't say no to me, and love my body no matter what. Hurt takes root and both feel vulnerable. Their vulnerability may be sensed by someone outside the relationship promising lots of sex. For the other, promises of being loved and cherished and accepted just as they are is what they need. Either way, it can be a pitfall. It is helpful to recognize these pitfalls in advance and understand what a normal level of frequency is for your partner before you make a lifelong commitment. Compromise is huge!

To avoid conflict, maybe one of them agrees to have sex even though they don't feel like it. This can be easier to hide for a female, since a man's desire is physically evident. If he is perceptive, he'll know, anyway, that his partner is not into it.

To sum it up, know what your other half's expectations are prior to your commitment. Discuss the triple F's and seek counseling if you are of different minds. This could help you sleep at night when you aren't tossing and turning from frustration. (Another F).

Don't take this chapter too seriously. It is simply something else to think about tonight. Think about getting old and earning the right to be set in your ways.

Chapter 36. Old People

Old people: we're all going to be one someday. …. Or, a politically correct way of saying that; *senior citizens, retirees, not-entirely-mobiles.*

I have always said that when I get old I'll still be active, have sex with my husband, and be nice. Who hasn't had to deal with a cantankerous old person? Did you ever say to yourself *that's not going to be me or heck ya that's going to be me: I earned it!*

There are many things that go south when you get old: one of them would be the ability to properly hear at a normal decibel level.

Let me give you a story of my recent experiences with senior citizens in my family.

My father flew out to visit for a family funeral: it was his younger brother who had died. He knew that it was necessary even though he does not like airports, can't hear what the flight attendants say, and he doesn't like driving on the Los Angeles freeways to transport himself to the airport in the first place. Nonetheless, he arrived and my sister and I willingly picked him up at the airport. Now I look exactly like my dad, all the way down to his very curly hair. In the recent past, I have worn my hair straight and fought the curls, mightily. However, on fly date, it was au naturale. My father walked through the gate where he met my sister and me. Mind you, I have not seen him in a year and he looks at me and says, "What happened to your hair?" I made a face to my snickering sister letting her know my displeasure at this apparently rude greeting. (She passed muster, by the way). Then, quickly followed by that he said, "Did anyone forget to tell you it's not Halloween?"

So, my dilemma: is he being offensive or is he merely exercising his right to express his opinion, or does he honestly think he's being funny? Is it because he's set in his ways and doesn't like change? Does he think it's funny because he has a sarcastic sense of humor? Well, I honestly don't know other than to say initially my feelings were hurt. I thought my curls were cute but after those comments, I doubted my confidence.

The next morning (we were all staying at my sister's home) after he woke up and walked into the kitchen, he took one look at me and said, "I hope you didn't pay good money for that." Seriously? What really rankled was that I had a hair appointment that day to get it blown out into silky straightness. All during my hair appointment I was feeling irritated; as if I had given into pressure. When I returned to my sister's house he said, "Your hair is straight: I hope it wasn't something I said!" With this senior citizen, I could not win! Perhaps you're still smoking mad at something a senior said to you and that's what is keeping you up on this night. Maybe you're totally relating to what I'm writing.

Another favorite topic of mine is my now 96 year old mother-in-law. It's weird to have a mother-in-law the same age as my grandma would have been, but she had my husband much later in life. He's accustomed to having a senior parent; for me it's still new. She lives on the other side of the country from us so we routinely fly out to see her in her retirement home. Her favorite thing to do is to treat my husband as if he is still a little boy. She finds ways to determine if I (not him) have given him balanced meals: meat, potatoes and vegetables. She'll say things on our frequent calls such as "So, what did you have for dinner tonight?" We have learned, interpreted that means, "Did you have a balanced meal?" If my husband says we had pizza, she'll slyly say, "Oh, and what kind of salad did you have with that pizza?" She inquires with such sweetness; you barely know you're being grilled.

Our big joke is for me to make gestures to ease my husband's tension. Her vision is not all that great nor is her hearing. When she babies my husband, I hold my arms in a cradling position pucker my lips and look down at my arms as I swing the imaginary baby back and forth. My husband will glare at me while his mother is oblivious to the fun we are making of her. Making fun is my coping mechanism. I adore her, so please don't think this is cruel. She is awesome!

On our last visit, we took her to the grocery store. There was somebody at the dairy case speaking a language I had never heard and apparently, neither had my mother in law. She loudly exclaimed with a smile plastered on her face, "Oh, no speaka da English?" I knew she was annoyed and I also knew my husband and I were horrified: I felt sick. "Clean-up in Aisle 7". Her heart is open to all people; she just gets frustrated when she can't understand the conversation and participate, too.

When we returned to the retirement home, she got her walker out and stated she was going to take us on a tour. (She wanted to show her baby boy off to the residents). The corridors were in a horseshoe pattern with rooms lining the halls much like a college dormitory would be. When we approached the cafeteria area, there was a little lady hunched over in her chair with a disheveled appearing wig on her head, chin down, muttering to herself. My mother-in-law's voice rang out loud and clear, "Oh, that's Margaret; she used to have her makeup on just right and her hair just perfect. Look at her now with no makeup, hair unkempt, saying mow mow mow mow mow." I could feel my face redden. I silently prayed that Margaret also would not comprehend what was just broadcast. The tour went downhill from there, believe me.......I'm too embarrassed to even write it. Mind you, my mother-in-law is as sweet as can be: it's just that hear hearing prevents her from understanding how loudly she speaks and she feels she has earned the right to speak without a filter.

Music is a universal language. While at the retirement home I was escorted to a piano in the hallway while my mother-in-law proceeded to tell the residents I played piano. So, I pulled out some music and began to play. (I do not play by ear, only with music). When I finished, I had drawn a crowd. There were some people thoroughly enjoying it while one old guy said, "Is that all you can play is that damned church music? Can't you play something more upbeat?" He had no idea I could only play what was in front of me. He wanted a saloon girl and I felt as if I should put a jar saying "tips" on top of the piano. What was it about old males? I struck out again!

When it was time for my husband and me to return to our hotel room, my mother-in-law asked me if it was okay to hug my husband. Then, she hugged him and proceeded to give him a neck massage. I began my cradling motion again.

Back to my dad: I could do chapters on him, but will try to limit this story. (I only want you up reading this as long as it takes to distract you from the thoughts interrupting your sleep.) My dad has a bad habit of chewing his tongue like a stick of Wrigley's Spearmint gum, the only kind he will chew. He makes smacking sounds as he rolls that big ole tongue around his gums, over his lips and then begins to chew it. Smacking slurping noises are like fingernails down a chalkboard to me. One night when he was visiting us we were playing Dominoes. We had a fire going in the fireplace and a cozy feeling in the room. The smacking, chewing and slurping soon commenced. I kicked my husband under the table trying to get him to share my pain, but he was oblivious as to why I was kicking him. Deciding to speak in code and also knowing my dad couldn't hear half of what I was saying, I began to tell stories to my husband, trying to get him to say the word, "Decker". Decker is my daughter's annoying dog that self gratifies himself with slurping noises that drive me up the wall. So, the game is going on and I say, "Honey, remember when we were living in England and we rode those red tour buses in London? The ones with the ah bottom and the open top? The ah ah ah double??..." Right on cue, he walks into it and says "Decker?"

I started choking back my laughter as I said "yes, yes, that's it". My husband is not catching on still. I knew it was going to take a while. So, I began anew, thoroughly enjoying this game I was playing within the game. My dad was studying the dominoes, and rolling that tongue as if there were no tomorrow.

"Honey, remember when our daughter wanted to open that business in Los Angeles with the ice cream sandwiches? What was that place called?" Helpfully he says, "Decker's?" Laughter is erupting from me as tears roll down my face. I'm trying not to let my dad see so I am practically spluttering. By now my husband is suspicious but still not quite with me. I tried one last time to drive home the point.

"Honey, what about those sandwiches we had at that deli? They were stacked with two kinds of meat and a piece of bread in between: what was that? A turkey grinder? No, a um double ah,…"

…."Decker?" he supplies? Now, understanding has dawned and he bursts into laughter, quickly catches himself and my dad finally looks up. We caught his attention, but didn't want to hurt his feelings, so we took deep gulping breaths and said we were just reminiscing. I literally was choking on spasms of laughter. My husband was less successful and the tears quickly ran down his face. My dad was clearly looking puzzled, adding to my sense of guilt.

I now had someone to share my annoyance with and somehow that tongue smacking became bearable. I just needed patience with my elderly dad and humor was the way I obtained it.

Now back to the family gathering at my sister's and the funeral. My dad's older brother was too infirmed to make it to the funeral. Since my dad lived so far away he rarely saw his brothers. My dad being the fair-minded person he was flew into the northern part of the state where the funeral and my sister were and then had his return ticket from my city, 4 hours away. I offered to drive him to his older brother's house and go 2 hours out of my way when we returned to my city just to get him there. I knew it was important the two remaining brothers had time to visit.

The entire way to his brother's house he had his hearing aid turned down in the car (because the background noise interfered with the hearing aid), but he talked my ears numb for 6 hours. (That doesn't include the time at his brother's house). I reminded myself that someday I would give my right arm to hear him tell his stories so I determined to treasure the time rather than resent it. It was an exercise in patience.

We arrived at my aunt and uncle's house where I bought gluten free pizza and alternately watched 3 senior citizens turning their hearing aids up and down and listening to the whirring whining sound they made when amplified too much. When they didn't understand each other, they locked eyes, nodded their heads and muttered, "Yup."

After lunch, I got my dad back in the car for the rest of the trip. I was his captive audience. And talk about not knowing your audience: senior people in my family just talk about themselves and their interests. For 6 blasted hours I heard about farming, farm implements, how much per acre it cost in the 60's to lease a plot of land, and how to tune up a car. He got onto one interesting topic about playing cork ball in the streets. I guess they would use a thermos as a bat after removing the cork which was screwed into the drinking portion beneath the cup. The cork became the ball and thermos street ball would begin. And **that** was the highlight of the conversation. It was all I could do to keep my eyes on the road. At the end of the trip, we got out of the car and he said, "I'll bet you were glad to have me along: I kept talking so I could keep you awake and we're here in one piece, so it looks like it worked." What did I do? I smiled! (Dad if you're reading this I love you!)

To sum up old people: they can be hard of hearing, have difficulty seeing, repeat themselves incessantly, chew their tongues, reminisce, be unyielding in their schedules, (Late show at 10pm, news at 7am, cheese and crackers at noon), but annoying or not, they have paid their dues and we will soon be there ourselves. So how do I deal with it? With grace sprinkled with a whole lot of humor! So much humor, in fact, that the next chapter is dedicated to the old guys swapping stories after the funeral.

Chapter 37. Tale of the Two Furbies

This is a very short chapter: if you only need a jump start, this chapter is for you.

My father and his brother-in-law were reunited. They had not seen each other in over 30 years. Both are old farmers at heart. They decided to spend an evening catching up. These two dear gentlemen are both hard of hearing yet they were determined to swap farm stories. There were a lot of "remember whens" with heads leaned in toward each other in earnest conversation. (The leaning was more to the fact they couldn't hear rather than anything else.) Now my father can talk and talk and talk, but my uncle can do circles around him. I sat and watched the two of them, seeing the frustration mounting on my dad's face when he couldn't hear every word nor get a word in edgewise. My uncle was much more proficient at keeping the chatter going. He is a charming gregarious gentleman who is irresistible in any setting: so much to talk about!

I sat there watching them and began to recall a similar story that creates the best analogy for this scene. The more I watched, the funnier it got.

Do you remember the Furbies that originally were released for sale in 1998? They are those little owlish looking furry stuffed animal-like robots? The Furbies did not speak English, but rather were programmed with a language called Furbish. It was the owner's job to train the Furby and teach it English. The repetitive sounds were captured by the Furby, which would then repeat the new words back. It was tons of fun for kids (and us adults) to train our little robotic pets.

We ended up purchasing a Furby for our son's birthday. It was such a smash; we ended up getting a second one (for my husband---not kidding). My son had done a decent job training his Furby to speak. Once it was switched on, we could count on (we'll call him Furby #1) to chatter away. He did not disappoint.

My husband's Furby (Furby #2), was not catching on very well at all to the English language. He kept blurting out things like "A-Tay", (hungry), "Boh-Bay", which meant worried and "Way-Loh" (sleep) right before it would literally nod off and snore. Furby #2 snored much more than Furby #1. As any good robotic pet owner would attest to, if your robot is not learning, then you must show it an example of a success story; Furby #1.

The two geniuses' (my son and husband) conferred and decided it would be a great idea if Furby #1 would train Furby #2. They figured that if they turned the Furbies on in the morning before we all left, put them face to face so they could sense the other one, it would be the perfect atmosphere for Furby #2 to learn. When they returned that night, Furby #2 would have a new vocabulary. The first thing we did was woke them up. All seemed to be going well; Furby #1 was chattering away, Furby #2 was speaking Furbish, slowly, and we were all giggling, excited about their impending progress.

Can you guess what the outcome was? Furby #1 blew Furby #2's brains right out of its little robotic head. Furby #2 had short-circuited. We diagnosed this demise as overloaded brain syndrome. Furby #1 quite simply talked Furby #2 to death.

Now fast forward to the two farmers reuniting face to face at the kitchen table. The frustrated look on my dad's face began to change over the period of a couple hours. My uncle (Furby #1) was still animatedly talking about 6 bottom plows, the upper 40, the old John Deere, and the flood of 68. I noticed my dad's eyes were glazing over and his chin was drooping. His contribution to the conversation had ceased. Furby #2 was about to implode: time for me to step into the rescue.

End of story: time for you to "Way-Loh". Night night!

Chapter 38. Funerals

Have you ever lost someone close to you and attended their funeral and/or memorial? There are so many ways families and friends offer remembrance to their dearly departed, I can't list them all. By now you'll understand I handle stress through humor. Maybe you think that is insensitive, sacrilegious, and just plain morbid. Perhaps you'll understand a case of the nerves. Certainly no one can say they enjoy the death of a loved one or acquaintance.

I know I am constantly reminding you that this book is about insomnia, but I don't want you to forget. The point for these chapters is to distract you. With that in mind, you most assuredly have experienced nighttime ruminations about the death of someone you knew.

Aren't there so many different ways to demonstrate remembrance? It largely depends on religion, area of the world, how close families/friends are, finances, and traditions.

When I lived in the Southwestern part of the country, Mariachi's were not unusual to have at a funeral. The casket would be solemnly carried up the church aisle by 6 pallbearers while the Mariachi's followed woefully singing their songs. The "Ava Maria" is a well- known song that petitions a deep emotional response. Mariachis are also used at gravesides; their music echoing the heartfelt feelings of those gathered.

When someone dies, family members will either carry out the wishes of the deceased or ignore them and do it their way for whatever reason; could be financial. Cremation, memorial service, no memorial service (some refer to as the Wake or Viewing the night before the funeral), what to do with the ashes, if there's to be a church ceremony, a memorial; no ceremony at a church, graveside service, etc. The list is as varied as the people who plan the events.

Surely we have all thought about when our time comes and what it should look like. Some of us will be more open to the discussion than others, but it's certainly crossed all of our minds. I always felt it was important to ask my family members what their wishes were. Some families will have the funeral all pre-paid and pre-planned by the loved one who has passed. In these situations, all you have to do is pick out the coffin or urn for them. It is possible coffin preparations were done by the decedent in advance, if their death was expected. So, you get my drift: I could talk about many of these situations, but will stick to just a few for the express purpose of brevity.

When my mother died, she had already selected her headstone and gravesite. However, the rest of the details were left to my dad, sister and I. It was like purchasing a new car when selecting the casket. Did we want sealed or unsealed; there was a vault and they were also sealed or unsealed. What color dress was she wearing and would we like to see the interior to determine if it would match? We were shown springy mattresses and ones without give. It was overwhelming and hard to deal with in such an emotional state.

In the framework of morbid humor, I'm going to discuss a funeral where the person dies, there's a viewing at the funeral home followed by a funeral the next day at either a church or the funeral home.

Have you ever been the family member, standing in the receiving line in front of the open casket as well-wishers file by to express their sympathy and swap stories? Do you feel the hair on the back of your neck prickle? Do you think the body will move, reach out, tell you your shirt's un-tucked, or tap you on the shoulder? Have you ever imagined you saw the body twitch? Do you stare at them thinking they really do look like clay and not how you remembered them? Like me, do you get distracted by obscure things, such as that's not how they combed their hair: it was parted on the side, not in the middle, or I don't remember that watch on their wrist! Silly random thoughts. When he was alive, I never would have taken the liberty to simply stare at his face; it would have been downright weird.

What do I do when I'm nervous? I talk and way too much. I chatter, make stupid jokes all the while hearing a voice in my head saying "Shut-up KC: shut-up: you're babbling": The little devil on my other shoulder is responding "I can't, I can't, I can't: I just can't!" So, I stare and I blurt out, "Why, he's got my earlobes! Would you just look at them? He should have had piercings, too. Those lobes could hold at least 5 earrings!" I'm mortified by my comment and the little voices war within me. "I didn't realize his hair was so curly, too: I had no idea how much alike we look!" Wait a minute, does that mean I'm saying I look like a corpse? The thought seems inappropriate even typing it.

Viewings can be family reunions. When I saw cousins I hadn't seen since I was a kid, I began to blather on and on. I couldn't shut up: I just talked and talked. I became Furby #1. When I left the viewing, I was appalled at my behavior. Why was I chatty? What an idiot I am. It was because I was nervous!

Others when nervous will clam up: they will file by the coffin, proffer their hand in a heartfelt handshake to the closest family member, say a few brief words, carefully walk on past the casket without going too slowly, proceed to a seat in the room, where they will remain, quietly taking in the somber reason for being there.

All the while people like me are chatting in subdued whispers on the sidelines as the sitters are probably thinking the talkers are very disrespectful. I recall feeling that way myself when I was a young girl and had to stand by my mother's coffin while people laughed and joked in the room: I was deeply offended because I did not have a clue as to how the human psyche worked.

I have also seen what I call the toucher. Some people are predisposed to touch the body; it can be a feather light touch of the loved one's hand, a kiss to the forehead or more. Then there's the thumper. I have literally seen someone pat the chest of the departed so rapidly that the hollow body sounds could be heard and the corpse slightly rose up and down in the coffin with each thump. I guess that casket had a springy mattress.

Last, we'll close this chapter out by speaking about the graveside ceremony. Whether your loved one was in a casket or an urn, there still can be an interment at a cemetery. Sometimes there may be disagreements between family members about whether or not to stay while the coffin or urn is lowered into the ground. It is so final and many prefer to stand by the graveside, have a prayer or two, maybe a song, and then leave. It is all a matter of preference and understanding how the one who died would have wanted it.

When my 94 year old father in law died, a Scottish pre-paid funeral had been planned. My husband and I, along with his siblings did all we could: got the flowers, assured the obituary was correct, wrote notes for the eulogy, picked out his suit and delivered it to the funeral home and assisted my mother in law with speaking to the funeral director. The children all decided we should have a bagpipe player at the graveside. My mother in law wanted us to all be gathered while the casket was lowered into the ground: the bagpipes were to play as this was occurring. This was a logical procedure to her. We wanted every wish to be granted to comfort her during this deep time of sorrow.

Well, nothing goes without a hitch in our lives. Right before the funeral began, a panicked funeral director pulled me into an ante room where she proceeded to tell me they couldn't bury my father in law because the doctor had not signed the death certificate. Think about that; how would you have handled such a dilemma? The funeral was about to begin, my mother in law was seated in the front pew, the bagpipers were outside waiting for the coffin to be brought out, and I absolutely knew this was not information they could deal with when emotions were so raw. So I did what any level headed chatty Kathy would do. I pulled my husband to the side and told him there would be a change of plans and to just go with it. I told the bagpipers to start playing when I nodded to them as soon as the minister had prayed after the 23rd Psalm. I said only that we decided not to be present when the casket was lowered into the ground.

At the end of the funeral, we escorted my mother in law over the uneven ground to the graveside and seated her under the tent facing the coffin. We rallied around, heard the prayers, the bagpipes rang out their sorrowful strains, and then the funeral folks went back to the building following my lead as I stood up and headed that way. We ushered family members into a family photo away from the coffin and escorted my mother in law back to the building post-photos. She never questioned it; we just took charge and it didn't even occur to her that we had changed anything. I'm not sure she even noticed the casket was still on the dais.

Sometimes you have to withhold information as an act of compassion. I knew she could not have handled him being in that coffin inside the funeral home all night long. She would have wanted to have it out with the powers that be and experienced undue stress and drama she did not need to be subjected to.

Mercifully, the certificate was signed the next morning so that by the time she went to visit the grave, all was well. We squeaked by: sometimes a little white lie in my opinion is okay if it spares the well-being of another person. I think we'll discuss white lies in the next chapter. This isn't a novel so don't keep reading unless you're still wide awake, but I suspect after discussing funerals, you may not feel like reading more until next time!

Chapter 39. White Lies

There's a card on my kitchen table. I want to send it to just the right friend who can appreciate the need for a small tale. On the front of the card is a picture of a girl looking at a donkey. The donkey has on a pair of jeans over its hind quarters. The caption says something to the effect of "Do these pants make my ass look fat?" We laugh because it's so true. How awful to be the person on the receiving end of that question: they may feel forced into telling a lie: a white lie.

I'm not going to go all philosophical on you, but I think we can look at what consists of a white lie. We can all agree it's a tiny lie: one that is meant not to harm but to protect. There are classic situations which many feel would call for a white lie. Let's list some of the common ones.

- Does my hair look okay?
- Do these glasses make me look old?
- Do these glasses make me look smart?
- Did you hear that? (as you passed gas)
- Does my ass look fat?
- Do I look too young; too old?

- Is that a wrinkle on my forehead?
- Can you see that big zit right in the middle of my face?
- Was my play really that bad during basketball?
- Do the others think I'm stupid?
- Was that gaff really that bad when I said such and such to so and so?
- Do I look my age?
- Could I pass for 21?
- Do you think they would card me?
- What do you think of my writing? (Don't answer that one; we writers are sensitive!)

The philosophical debate is timeless. When is it okay to tell a white lie? Is a white lie really a lie? It's a commandment, right? "Thou Shalt Not Lie!" It's an oath you take in a courtroom with your right hand on the Bible while stating "I promise to tell the whole truth the full truth and nothing but the truth". There is no *except when* sprinkled into those oaths.

We can back up and rationalize a bit while we're formulating the lie. Isn't holding harmless the key here? If our answer does not harm anyone, then is it really so bad? Do you tell a lie by omission?

Doesn't it make sense to spare somebody's feelings such as in the fat questions? My answer is, I honestly don't know! Justification: what thought process did you go through to decide to lie? Did you do a quick brain surf and rapidly conclude that this person needs a boost and now is not the time to affirm their belief that they let themselves down? After all, there are many reasons for being overweight; some medical. The old don't kick somebody when they're already down? Your motive is to encourage?

If you tell a white lie will it enable a person to go on with the illusion that everything is just peachy when it's not? Will your lie keep them on a path they should maybe turn from?

What about if it's their choice of partner? They want your opinion, but you don't want to be the bad guy. But what if that person is all wrong for them yet you pretend to be encouraging anyway by saying something like "If you're happy, then I'm happy for you!" Could that lie be wrong if you're really thinking "You could do a lot better and that person is not as into you as much as you may think." As I write this, the truth seems kinder in the long run.

I have a friend who went out on a date with a guy and when she came home she looked in the mirror and noticed a tiny piece of lettuce stuck between her teeth. Horrified, she called me up and asked me if I thought he noticed it and why wouldn't he say something? So, I answered, "Oh no, I'm sure he didn't notice unless you smiled super wide: it wasn't between your middle teeth, right? He would have said something, I'm sure." Did I really believe that to be the case? Probably not! But I didn't want to make my friend feel worse than she already did.

Yesterday I was at a function where my friend evidently forgot to put eyeliner on her other eye. It distracted me several times seeing one outlined eye while the other remained naked. Did I say something to her? I didn't, because I couldn't think how to say it without embarrassing her. Yet you may say, I should have told her and I would agree. I'm not sure this fits into the white lie category unless you think this would be a lie of omission.

Last year I was at a business meeting where some experts were flown in to give a presentation to a lofty group of surgeons. She was an expert in her field and confident about her topic. When she entered the conference room she did not know that the exact center button of her blouse was undone. Someone pointed it out to her in front of God (because some surgeons do have the god-syndrome) and everybody. This poor lady became so flustered and thoroughly embarrassed that her whole presentation tanked! I still ask myself if it was right that it was publically pointed out, or if it could have been handled differently. This was a situation where I would have pulled her to the side and said, "You might want to button that there before you continue your presentation." And then when she asked if I thought everybody else had noticed, I would look her right in the eye and say "Absolutely not: I just happened to notice because of the angle of where I sat." Even if she was in the middle of that presentation I would have found a way to get her out of the room for a second and away from eyes that would embarrass her. To me that white lie would be a kindness: a merciful act.

How about the kid who's always picked last and comes home crying to their parents because they feel bullied or unworthy? When they ask you if they're truly that awful at sports what should you do; say "yes, yes you really are that bad?" I couldn't do that. I would find a way to maybe tell a little white lie to build them back up but still not completely lie so that they start thinking they're really super-duper good. Maybe gently lead them to the fact that it doesn't matter what other kids say. That really is a slippery slope, though.

Think of the singing competition reality TV shows out there. At the beginning of each season, the producers feature acts that did not make it through. These people appear to think that they sing very well. They often times say that their grandma or dad or mom or somebody has always told them so. Their friends tell them, too. In those cases the little white lies can build a false sense of security where in actuality it would have been kinder to tell them the truth. "I know you enjoy singing, but I'm not sure it's your wheel house: why don't we look for your strong points and focus on those instead?"

I must mention that many of you ascribe to the proverb "Faithful are the wounds of a friend." I like to hear the truth but only from my friends: they are the ones who sprinkle love and acceptance all around it.

So in conclusion, what I got out of this whole debate with myself is this. It's all about your motive and the result. If your motives are pure, you're probably not going to steer anyone wrong. If your motives are self-serving, then you'd better take a pause and give it some more thought.

Chapter 40. Bowling and Golf

Our friends Ronny and Michelle occasionally like to bowl and golf: two of the most boring things to watch on television. Now if you're enthusiasts as they are, you still might agree. If you're an uber-enthusiast you may take great offense by that opening statement.

When Michelle met Ronny he was playing golf every single weekend. She thought that was nonsense. First of all, it sure didn't seem like exercise, although Ronny liked to bill it that way. He said if you forego the golf cart, then walking is great. (Start stop, start stop is how Michelle viewed it: no aerobics!) And, ever the considerate person, Michelle worried about the group of golfers behind them that were driving a cart. Wouldn't they see this walking from hole to hole as an unnecessary delay for their turn?

Second, how could clubbing a ball around 18 holes be exciting? There's so much time spent waiting for your next turn. If you had a new golfer in your group, the likelihood was there was they would miss par and then bogey, creating even more time between holes.

Yes, there is a language to golf; terms unique to the sport.

You've probably all heard of a "hole in one" or Ace. That's when you get the job done in one swing. The ball rolls or lands right into that little hole in the ground with just one swing. Awesome!

Eagle: Eagle means your score card reflects that you made two less shots than the experts say it requires to get your ball into the hole. (The predicted shot per hole is called Par). If you're not on "par" with Eagle, then maybe you made a bogey. Bogey meaning you scored one more swing than you wanted: one over par. (Ronny had many of these on his scorecard much to his dismay: even worse was when Michelle, newer to the game, could hit par once in a while.)

The last score phrase I'll give you is Birdie. Birdie is the opposite of Bogey. In this case, your score will reflect that the golfer actually scored one less than par.

For the fortunate, someone may carry your clubs for you, making themselves your caddie. Michelle did this for Ronny in the beginning because she wanted to observe the game, figure out which club they used for which kind of shot, etc. Observing can be a great way to learn.

Chip shots are meant to be short shots. (It gets complicated with how low to hit and how far away from the hole-cup-it is.)

The ball and clubs are considered your gear necessary for accuracy in the game. Club selection depends on how far and how high and from where you're hitting the ball such as on the green or from a sandpit. The balls have indentations in them called dimples. Scientific research figured out how many dimples it would take to make a ball fly straight and accurately.

Michelle and Ronny are competitive people. Even though Michelle didn't understand golf in the beginning, she became a fan because the challenge to get that little ball into the little cup was too great to resist. And, it gave her time with Ronny, although sometimes he preferred not having her along; in particular when her scorecard had lower numbers than his!

They also tried disc golf which was much more to Michelle's liking. The discs were weighted and categorized by putters (short shots), mid-range, and long-range. They even had discs that would compensate if your throw was too far to the right and the reverse. Although it was free to disc golf in local parks, they found themselves golfing with clubs much more than with discs.

Now if you like golf, then maybe you won't mind it on television, but Michelle admits this is boring beyond belief. Ronny likes it because he studies the swing of the professionals. But to Michelle the announcers' voice just drones on in their whispered slow speech. She only looks up at the television when she hears the smattering of applause from the crowd showing their appreciation of a particularly good shot.

Even more boring is watching the sport of bowling on television. Who does that? Well evidently quite a few people since the bowling tournaments were still being televised. Bowling is an engaging addictive sport in person, but not so much on television: not nearly as fun to watch unless the person has an outrageous form when rolling the ball down the lanes. (Think Fred Flintstone doing his twinkle toe run to the lane.) The lanes are about 60 feet long and 41 or so inches wide.

Ronny and Michelle are serious bowlers. They like the sport because it elicits an immediate result. Bowling alleys in this computerized world keep track of the score for the bowlers. Each stand where the balls are housed is shared between two lanes. The lanes are where you throw the ball to knock over your pins. The score is divided into frames. For purposes of this discussion, we'll talk in the context of ten-pin. There are ten pins or heavy objects lined up in a pattern with a head pin in front. We won't even go into that. The assumption is that you know what it looks like.

On the side of each lane is a gutter: you want to avoid the gutter at all costs. When someone throws a gutter ball, they miss the pins altogether and get a zero in their column. Each time up to roll the ball gives you two opportunities to knock the pin over. If you have a strike (all 10 pins down on first roll) or spare (all 10 pins down by your second roll) in the 9th frame then you get a bonus throw in that 10th frame. (Frames, by the way, are how many times you are up to bowl in a given game).

Since the computer is keeping score for you, the totals are always up on the screen for each frame. If you are fortunate enough to get a strike or a spare then there is a point system that allows for the bowler to pick up additional points in the next frame. In those cases, your total score won't show until the next frame. If you bowled a spare, then you would add 10 to the first score of the next frame. Michelle complains to Ronny on a frequent basis that the scoring is much too complicated and that if it wasn't for the computers automating this process, she'd just plain give up.

Ronny and Michelle have their own bowling balls because of the weight and the holes. The heavier the ball combined with a good release the more likely you'll be to take out more pins. If your ball is light weight and/or if you have a slow release then more pins will stand firm.

Because Michelle doesn't have dainty little fingers and her knuckles are large, the bowling balls provided by the alley do not work for her. The holes large enough to fit her fingers are on balls meant for man sized hands. In other words; they're too heavy. This may not be the case for all women, but it is for Michelle. To correct this problem, Michelle bought her own ball and had holes drilled specific to the size of her fingers: the bottom hole being for her thumb and the two top holes for her index and middle fingers. By having a custom ball she was able to pick the weight comfortable for her. Whenever she used the heavier balls, she would get a lump in her forearm from the stress on her tendons.

The same went for Ronny: he wanted a ball whose weight was customized to his forearm strength. The additional benefit for them was that they could have a unique color or design on their ball so that when it rolled back up into the counsel from the pin area, they could pick it out of the group in their lanes.

To sum it up, golf and bowling are games where you not only compete against others but you can make it your goal to ignore them and simply do your personal best. If you golfed significantly over par, then your goal may be to whittle two swings off the next time out. If you bowled a 60 (which Michelle has done from time to time), then your goal may be to add a few more strikes onto that scoreboard.

Speaking of strikes, have you ever had a strike in the personal sense? Or, struck out? Well, I did when I was introduced to life at a dog park.

Chapter 41. Secret Life of a Dog Park Dweller

Ron and I were excited. Finally, we were going to be dog owners. It all started when we entered a local hardware store and walked straight into the most ginormous Great Dane we had ever seen. He was fawn colored, with big floppy ears, huge black jowls, sporting a red bandana around his huge neck. His name was Otto and he was so sweet.

Immediately upon returning home we began to surf the internet until we found a litter of Great Danes almost ready for release. We gave our new puppy a stately name; Gertie. Her dad was 170 pounds while her mother weighed in at a dainty 165 pounds. (Watch out Otto).

Gertie arrived at 8 weeks old already weighing in at 19 pounds. Once she had received all her shots she was pronounced old enough to interact with other dogs. Since we lived in the desert, our yard did not have any grass; just bumpy hot rocks. Desiring to see our rambunctious too energetic puppy run off steam, we scoped out the nearest dog park. She needed playmates.

Have you ever been to a dog park? We had not and so we had no idea we were about to enter an entirely new realm; an alternate world.

On our first day at the park, we felt like new parents delivering our child to its first play date. The park had two fenced areas, divided by a 10 foot free space. There was the small dog fenced play yard (less than 30 pounds) and the 1 acre fenced area for large dogs. A few mesquite trees were scattered around the park for shade, inadequate though they were.

Inside the fenced area under a tree was a spigot and a 5 gallon bucket for water. (The Golden Retrievers liked to have 1 foot in those buckets as they drank.) At the middle of the play area near the perimeter was a concrete picnic table along with various plastic porch chairs scattered about. On the near side of the park was another large concrete picnic table, placed in the middle.

We walked in with fear and trepidation. Gertie, on the other hand was just the opposite; quivering from head to toe with anticipation. The far picnic table and chairs were filled with white haired people with heads leaned in talking in earnest tones while making tsking sounds. A portable radio blared out biased political opinions. Standing up against the fence behind them were several big young single guys and a few girls. Everyone appeared to know each other's names, all of the dog's names, and who belonged to whom.

The table in the mid-section closest to the entrance had a lone young single guy, his dog separated from the pack. And pack there was! The rest of the dogs, about 10 in all, were literally running in formation, clearly following an alpha male shaggy black haired dog. A man with an expensive camera stood amongst them rapidly shooting photos.

We wandered over to the group of dog owners and introduced themselves while the others asked 20 questions about Gertie: why did we have a pure bred dog, how old was she, where did she come from, why did we choose a Dane, how much did she weigh, did she have her dog license, her shots, and on and on. It felt like the inquisition.

After the grilling, we quickly understood there were rules to follow. You must keep your dog under control, *unlike Bonnie, they said, who lets her dog attack theirs and thinks it is harmless fun!* We were told dogs must be kept on a leash when outside the fenced area and were asked if Gertie was leash trained.

Gertie embraced this pack of dogs and excitedly tried to nuzzle all her new playmates. They, however, did not entirely appreciate her greeting and growled, knocked her down, got her on her back and nipped at her neck and haunches. We didn't know what to think about this, so we kept a close eye, cautious that our baby might be hurt. One dog drew blood. Ron had enough, but still didn't want to offend the other owners so graciously he waylaid Gertie and attempted to leash her. Well, puppy that she was (60 pounds at that time), she shook Ron off as if she were a pitcher silently communicating with a catcher at a major league baseball game. Off she went with a light in her eyes that clearly said *Come Get me! Chase: Yippee!* And yes, the white hairs began tsking their disapproval. Comments flew across the yard: *You need to get her to obedience school, she could use a dog psychologist, and you need to bring treats to coax her to you: chicken is the best! And while you're at it, get her snake trained to make her more wary.*

So like any husband/wife team, we decided to divide and conquer. We humbly accepted a piece of chicken from a nice patron and tempted Gertie over to us with the offering. Gertie came running along with the entire pack. I grabbed and Ron leashed. (More tsking: Yes, we know, we need to bring snacks and then have enough for all the other dogs: we must not be rude!) And this was only our first time out. We were daunted.

I was on my own on the weekdays since Ron's work schedule didn't allow for an hour at the dog park. And Gertie was insistent in the mornings that it was time to go play: she'd paw and paw at me and beg with her eyes. Who could resist?

Gertie had immense anticipation for her romps in spite of the dominant dogs and she remained so full of spunk that I begrudgingly returned to the dog park each time she begged. Selfishly I conceded that I had a nice tired puppy upon return and that maybe it was worth it, so I kept going. The second time wasn't so bad; the people remembered Gertie and offered up a spare seat at the picnic table. Maybe I'd broken into the dog park clique.

It didn't take long before a vocal owner of another Dane expressed her distaste at the way the owner of two Golden Retriever puppies had brought a tennis ball for them to fetch; only for her dogs. *She's not sharing and that's not safe* comments began circling around the table. I was confused: wasn't that why dogs were brought to the park? And then as if to underscore it, her dog ran to chase the ball down and Retriever lady yelled at the dog to back off. Dane lady shouted out a loud comment about how if you're going to bring toys then you need to expect that they'll be shared. Retriever lady ignored her as if she were a pesky gnat which only served to annoy Dane lady even more. To me, Dane lady had common sense!

The Dane lady (whom I learned to lean on and found very supportive and helpful) had a support group just like Retriever lady did. Those protective folks decided to take their dogs into a fenced baseball field just behind the dog park area. Since it was fenced and the owners all brought clean-up bags to extract their doggies' leavings, they felt it would be no big deal. So, off they went. Gertie was invited to join but at that point I tactfully said it was about time Gertie went home anyway. I was not about to choose sides this new to the game.

Well, life went on in this fashion for quite a while. When a tiff happened, the vocal people would take their dogs over to the baseball field. Sometimes there were as many dogs in the baseball field as there were in the dog park. The owners were very careful to rake the dirt around the pitcher's mound back into its neatly groomed manner and since there weren't any baseball games going on during the weekday mornings, life was good. Whenever we saw the divide, we were conflicted as to where we should take Gertie. Her favorites were at the baseball field, but the dog park was the place where we *should* go. I'm a dot your I's cross your T's, follow the rules sort of girl. (At first I typed that "dog" your I's. Freudian slip?

One morning I gave into the temptation to use the baseball field and so I joined the others when they called out to Gertie. It was a great decision! Gertie was in her element. And then the drama started. Someone dared to bring a ball into the area and threw it across the field. Two dogs joyfully ran after the ball from separate directions, each leaping into the air. With a huge thud they collided and fell to the ground. One of them immediately began vomiting red blood. A panicked owner scooped up the huge dog, while another kind owner volunteered to drive them to the nearest animal hospital. They found out it was a fractured rib that had punctured the dogs lungs.

Neither of the two dog owners were the ones who threw the ball, but the drama between the colliding owners began. The dog that did not get injured in the collision was now the target of injured owner's derision. He felt Uninjured dog owner should pay the vet bill, others thought the person who brought the ball was at fault, while people like me felt it was an unfortunate accident.

The next weekend that we went to the dog park, camera guy was back. He kindly introduced himself and began taking shots of Gertie. He said he had created a website for dogs called "Butt Book". Proudly he announced that Butt Book was his way of providing social media to dogs. Each dog got a page with action shots from their park adventures. Gertie had made it into the site: We had reached the inner circle.

Once we had entered into the inner sanctum of Butt Book and the baseball field with Gertie, life at the dog park became simpler. (It was expected that dog names could be memorized by us if Butt Book was used appropriately: we now had homework). It became easier for us to tune out all the cliquish behaviors. We became very attached to Dane lady because she made a lot of sense and our dogs were best buds.

One day there was a riff about the placement of one of the picnic tables: how could anyone leave it in the middle where the dogs could run into it when they weren't looking? A couple of big guys thought it would be a good idea to move it against the perimeter like the other concrete one was. So, with good intentions all around, they heaved the monstrosity near a fence and widened the open area for the dogs. Innocent enough, right? Oh no: a big No Way!

The white hairs came into the park and saw the table had moved. Mind you, it was not the table they sat at: this was the table the lone owner would sit on. But it had MOVED!!!! Outraged comments began to circulate amongst the white haired owners seated in their plastic seats and other concrete table. I secretly thought it was hilarious since I just love observing people. While the white hairs were griping, they were sitting on a couple chairs that earlier had been marked by a couple of the male dogs. The yellow puddle stains still there. I got a kick out of that! I guess you could say I had passive aggressive thoughts and felt they deserved their unknown pee puddles.

At this point we decided to saunter over to the baseball field and join a couple other quieter dogs that were running back and forth as if their life depended on it. We needed to escape the drama. Gertie was ecstatic! Before long we noticed a white animal control vehicle slowly pull up and park outside the baseball field. Clipboard in hand, the animal control officer approached the field. *Do you have leashes and dog licenses?*

Dog licenses, I thought?

Yep, we owners were told to leash their dogs. This did not go over well with Dane lady and Lawyer man: They argued, *The dogs are in a fenced area!* Animal control man said that there were signs posted (he pointed to the back of a little 9" x 9" sign posted to one tiny spot of the baseball field). It said *Dogs must be leashed except in the dog park.* Each dog thankfully had a tag on them so that Animal control guy could document (or dogument?) that they were in an unauthorized area. He claimed there were complaints and judging by the group of onlookers gaping at us from the dog park area, the assumption was that Retriever lady may have turned us all in.

Adding injury to insult, we all had to provide our drivers licenses and phone numbers. The dogs now all had rap sheets.

So before you're yawning away, let us summarize about what life at a dog park entails:

Be prepared to join a clique.

Defend your dog always.

Read the signs even if they are only 9" x 9": make it a scavenger hunt to find them.

Try to remain neutral.

Your doggie isn't perfect even if you like to think so.

If you sit too long, Dominant male dog will pee on your leg.

Know the name of a good obedience school and throw it out there when asked who is training your dog.

Be prepared to have some petty cash: dog owners like to take their furry babies to dog friendly cafes after play.

If your dog drinks water, make sure you fill up the bucket.

If your dog drinks water with one foot in the pail, remove the mud and refill it for the others who require clean drinking water unless you want the wrath of the white hairs.

Respect the hierarchy: i.e. make a petition to move the tables before doing so.

Don't bring toys you do not intend to share.

Do not bring snacks unless there are enough for all the dogs.

Carrots aren't popular; (ask Carrot lady).

Get used to your dog being slimed by dogs with big jowls.

Make sure you go on Butt book and like or else Photo man is offended.

Divide the love.

Don't gossip nor engage with Lawyer man proudly known as Marxist owner: (seriously)

Ignore the political comments on Radio owner's battery powered radio.

Teach your dog to come: so much less embarrassing than corralling a wild horse.

Always clean up after your dog and immediately so it is not stepped in.

If someone doesn't clean up the poop, do it yourself and make tsking noises.

Time your visits to align with other like-minded dog owner's schedules.

Remember that the under 30 pounders must be referred to as the Yappers.

Learn how to make clucking noises with your tongues to relate to the Tskers. It's original.

And most importantly, know the names of the other dogs: the owners will be endeared to you for the effort.

Oh, and don't trip over your dog; it's very embarrassing. Tsk Tsk Tsk.

Chapter 42: Embarrassing Moments

Yes we do, we all have them: life's humiliating, embarrassing and traumatizing experiences. Let me tell you, I have had plenty; it never stops. In fact, they're so embarrassing; you may blush and then decide this is late night reading after all. I'm surprised I don't have some permanent disorder as a result.

I had a handyman come over to look at some items that needed repair in our home. Since Ron remains too busy to learn the handyman tasks, it is necessity to hire someone out. Ron was busy at work so I agreed to have the guy come over and show him around. I had been painting so was in old sweats and my painting sweater. Even though this is quite random, when I paint during the wintertime I wear a ribbed tight turtleneck sweater. It stops the paint from dripping down my skin. We all agree; I have skewed logic!

After I met with the handyman I closed the front door and felt that something wasn't quite right. When I looked down I noticed the front clasp of my bra had come undone and that my boobs were not in their right place; headlights were showing and my girls were kind of pushed to the sides. I was mortified! Later I told Ron that the handyman received full marks for maintaining eye contact.

About the same time my close friend had an even more embarrassing moment. They had a realtor team, husband and wife, over to view their home for possible sale. The husband walked into the walk-in closet, noting its size, looking up and down at the shelves to assess their potential and remarked that it was neat that there even was a wardrobe mirror in there. My friend felt proud of the fact their modest closet may have selling potential. (I have to say "my friend" because she would kill me if I used her name.)

The next day my friend decided she would do laundry so she marched into the walk-in closet to grab the hamper. Much to her horror, when she looked down at the floor near the mirror she noticed her *personal massager* laying prominently on top of the box it had been delivered in: (giant sized, too, because that's what her husband thought would have the most fire power). Even though she claimed it had not been used, it certainly looked like it was by the way it was splayed out on the floor. (Full marks again to a customer who kept a poker face.) She said she thought maybe she wouldn't give the agent their listing after that because it was just too embarrassing!

Embarrassing moments; you may be recalling your own at this point. Have you ever noticed that some people just seem prone to them? Call it what you will and analyze it all you want, but it's true. Maybe the people are just in a rush so they don't take time to think through their next move.

My embarrassing moments started at age 5. Since my parents did not provide feedback as to why I was in trouble, I was left to puzzle situations out. While new in the neighborhood the older man (8 years old) next door asked me to come over by his front porch. He and his younger brother snickered and said "if you pull down your pants, we'll give you an M&M".

Well, let me tell you: M&M's were considered a luxury so down those pants went. It was my first mooning experience! Of course life being what it is, my mother made her appearance on my front porch at that very moment, took in the situation and began screeching my full Christian, middle and last names for all to hear. "Get over here this minute: NOW!"

Boy did I get in trouble although my embarrassment was more at being caught with my pants down than with the actual crime. I got an M&M and I made sure I swallowed it while running home. Later in life, my husband went to a large retailer, bought a case of individual M&M packets and made a habit of calling my name while dangling a bag of M&Ms in front of my face. I'll just leave it at that!

When I returned to college at a not so tender age, I was nervous. My first day on the campus had me feeling self-conscious that I was not sporting a pony-tail and 19 year old taught skin. To better blend in I thought I'd wear shorts and flip flops.

On top of everything else, I was nervous about getting lost on campus hampered by the inability to read directional maps on notice boards, and of not knowing anyone. Once the day progressed, though, I found my confidence building. I had managed to locate my first two classes without any issues. Now ensconced in my third class, I was feeling pretty good about my day and my earlier anxiety was dissipating.

Halfway through the class the professor called for a break. Seated front and center, I jumped up from my desk and headed past the lectern holding the professor's laptop. Somehow my flip flop caught the mouse cord under my toes and the entire system came crashing to the floor. (Why did he need a mouse anyway and at least use a wireless one?) Because I had been in the front, the entire class was behind me to witness my clumsiness. Muttering under my breath with the red trailing its way up my neck, I hastily gathered laptop, mouse and pad and placed them back on the lectern, patting them when I got them returned as if to say *nice girl, nice girl.* Thankfully nothing seemed to be harmed. Making a dash for the door, I went into a bathroom stall and put my forehead on the side willing myself to return to class which I did with an attitude that said, *I dare you to say one word; I dare you!*

To add insult to injury after I was leaving the campus for the day I ascended some wide concrete stairs. Wouldn't you know it; my flip flop caught the cement edge and spilled me face first. Seriously! I was beside myself. I vowed; no more flip flops to class.

Have you ever crushed on another person and wanted to impress them terribly? I did! On one particular outing I joined my youth group for an outdoor roller skating rink experience. Most of the kids skated better than me but it didn't hamper my efforts. I dressed in my cutest little outfit, showing off my legs, and whirled around the rink. I was certain that the cool guy in my group would soon ask me to couples skate.

When I'm nervous I have to pee, so before he approached me I thought I'd roll on over to the bathroom. (He was the one with the good smelling family scent; the son of our music director: he was gorgeous!)

I returned to the rink and made my laps confident he was looking at my legs which the bulky skates somehow offset. (Delusional?) Much to my chagrin one of my girlfriends yanked on the back of my shirt nearly toppling me over. She whispered (thankfully), in my ear that there was a long piece of toilet paper trailing behind me still stuck in my underwear. My confidence burst and I never did get that couples skate. To this day I am horrified by the spectacle I must have been. Gorgeous guys require lots of self-esteem from their admirers; with mine shot, I didn't stand a chance!

Have you ever been in a public place that is noisy and are forced to shout loudly to the person next to you? Ever have the music or chatter abruptly stop just when you're loudly declaring something not meant for public consumption? Or, have you fallen at a time you were meant to be graceful? I used to do this during gymnastics at school. My teacher would just shake her head. Back to falling......there's more than what you've already read.

Let me tell you about two such incidents of mine. The first one was when I was a guest pianist at an outdoor function. It was held in a secluded courtyard with a beautiful fountain in the center and lush grass all around. I completed playing and while the group politely applauded I pushed back the bench and proceeded to walk to my table, smiling my thanks to everyone for their appreciation. Well appreciate they did when my spiked heel punctured the soft dirt and pitched me to my knees. The polite applause became wolf whistles and thunderous! Not knowing what else to do, I curtsied and continued to my seat. Sometimes you just have to own it!

Another time I was asked to do some modeling at a local mall. I was instructed to be made up with a certain manufacturer's makeup line and dress in a high end clothing stores' ensembles. A dais was setup center mall for the models to amble down, pivot at the end, and return. This was repeated several times while the models hurried back to the store to put on the next outfit and accessories.

As you can imagine being a novice I was nervous. I have never been a girly girl or one who actually enjoys being gazed upon by strangers. I'm a girly tomboy. Silently I was cursing my friend for talking me into this. With this distracted thought foremost in my mind, I walked up the stairs, waltzed down the platform and then pivoted at the end. What I didn't account for was that the store's shoes were a wee bit too loose. I pivoted right out of those shoes and left one on the stage. In my haste to grab the shoe with my free foot and scoot it back I twisted my ankle. What was my only saving grace? The outfit had a hat with a veil pulled over my eyes: the crowd could not see the horror on my face as I sought to regain my composure and slip back into the shoe while pretending my ankle was solid.

There are so many stories that could be relayed I could make a mini-novel.

Another one that comes to mind is when Ron decided to take me to one of our favorite steakhouses. The place was very good, business-casual type dress, and typically had at least an hour wait to get in. Once we were at our table and seated, I began to relax. I thoroughly enjoyed eating and drinking what they had to offer. Predictably, the liquid made its way through me and I excused myself to go to the restroom. The place was huge and packed to capacity. I had the waitress point out the location where the bathrooms resided. When I approached the general area, I saw two doorways. I pushed open the doors and walked right into the busy kitchen.

Since I was still smarting from that mistake, I felt exposed. I hurried as I made my way back to the table. In keeping with the way I was dressed, I wore heels. The floors were made out of uneven flagstone. When I pulled my chair back to reseat myself, my heel slid on the flagstone and I missed my chair. I pasted a smile on my face, picked up my bruised ego and tried to act as if nothing happened. It's almost worse when people politely look away and don't acknowledge what they just witnessed.

Bathrooms do seem to be the source of many incidents: you're surely remembering your own as you read this.

When Ron and I were dining at a casual military base installation, I got up to go to the bathroom. While seated in my stall the door opened and another user came in. It was a tight two-stall room. I could see through the slits in the doors and noticed a one piece flight suit clad figure had walked in. I recognized it was a pilot: a MALE pilot and that he was peeing in the sink. Oh no, wait a minute, I thought: *that's not a sink!*

I quickly pulled my feet up so he wouldn't notice small feminine appendages and impatiently waited for him to finish while squeezing my eyes shut to block out the sight. But it was not meant to be, because the latch on the stall door wasn't all that tight and guess what slid open before I could slam it shut with my foot? The man faced a mirror and I froze: did he see me? I didn't know, because I reflexively threw my arms out to shut that door. He wasn't acting as if he saw me. I waited a couple minutes after he left before I cautiously snuck out of that bathroom looking neither left nor right and slunk back into my chair next to Ron. Awful!

How about accidentally copping a feel? That one is a guaranteed red-faced moment. I had lunch with my friend. The friend met up with me at a local big box store after having her annual mammogram. Inside the store major renovations were going on. While cruising through the electronics section, a huge crash sounded from the rafters far overhead. So I did what any normal person would: I jumped and grabbed my friend, only it was her boob I got; not her arm. Feeling once again like all I could do was own it, I quipped *"Yep, everything checks out just fine"*. My embarrassing moment ended with the two of us in fits of giggles.

I have an acquaintance from my son's school. She is a volleyball mom to two girls. Since she doesn't have a son she attends the boys' games too. She is a team favorite. The boys get a kick out of her and also like that she brings snacks to their games. Don't get the wrong idea: she is not a cougar. She is just an older lady with a quick wit.

One day she was visiting with the boys and told them she was having her first colonoscopy. She said she thought it might be fun to write an "M" on each butt check. That way, she said, when the doctor had her lay back and put her legs up, it would say "WoW". My son was a true fan of hers after that: she was so funny! Now I would find that to be one of my most embarrassing moments, because after I left the group of kids I would be slapping myself mentally for being so silly.

Everyone needs an embarrassing story about work. I had a co-worker: we'll say his name is Spike.

Bored To Sleep

This guy looks like ZZ top with his long beard and tattoos. He collects skulls and displays them and an American flag at his cubicle and he rides a Harley. When he roars into the office parking lot, the leather tassels are rocking in the wind, his black leather vest is snapped tight and his chaps are protecting his thighs. (Underneath he wears turquoise scrubs with a big floral shirt because it's a medical office; which somehow amuses me greatly.)

His appearance aside, Spike is a teddy bear: all scary on the outside but a total marshmallow on the inside. So one evening when I was out cruising with my son with the sun roof open and tunes playing on the radio, I was surprised to see Spike revving his engine at a stop light in the lane to the left of me. I was thrilled to see someone I knew in a city of 1 million people; particularly because I was new to the area. Enthusiastically rolling my window down, I waved to get his attention and yelled "Hey Spike"!

Hmm, he was ignoring me. I was confused; maybe he didn't hear me so I gustily waved my arms again with a cheesy grin on my face while attempting to gain his attention, which in fact I did. He looked tough as nails. He stared right into my face which is when I realized that was not Spike. By this time my son was embarrassed, subconsciously slinking down in his seat while I found myself stammering as I tried to explain *I'm not crazy!*

I declared, "It's a Harley for crying out loud, it has leather straps, and the guy is not wearing a helmet, has a long beard, and is wearing a black vest and chaps." It's kind of like me not knowing my cars as I remark, *well, it was a blue car: they all look alike.* Or, *it was Mustang yellow so all cars that color must be Mustangs!*

How in the world could I be mistaken? I gave myself a couple minutes, saw the humor in it and laughed out loud. It was contagious: my son began laughing uncontrollably with me. But the tale is not over. I decided it was so funny that at work the next day I shared the story with Spike. I did it at a staff meeting with all present, because I have a self-deprecating sense of humor.

Without batting an eye and with all sincerity, Spike said, "Oh that must have been Skidmark: people mistake us for each other all the time."

"Skidmark?" I said? "Does he have an issue with his laundry?" Laughter erupted but Spike didn't get it.

Spike ever the literal one went on to explain to me that Skidmark earned the name when he wiped out on his bike. (To Spike, he's a "brother" and they take their wipe-outs very seriously.) I couldn't help but thinking, *if you take it so seriously then why don't you guys wear helmets?*

When my husband returned from the Middle East, we were between duty stations. He met me at a hotel in the town I was currently working in. We had a romantic evening getting reacquainted. The hotel had a breakfast buffet, so before I went to work we ate there. My office was only 2 blocks away, so after breakfast I walked to work with a spring in my step and a big smile on my face. After I arrived I noticed that I was being watched carefully by the staff. I could see laughter behind the backs of their hands and discussions as if to say "who's going to tell her: paper rock scissors?"

Finally, I said, "what gives? What is going on here?"

Carefully one of them pointed to my sweater set. (I was the boss by then which explained their reticence.) It was on inside out: both pieces. Boy did the joking begin then. I felt myself turn as red as my sweater. I wanted to march away, shut myself in my office and curse myself for not looking in the mirror. I wondered what the people at the breakfast area thought?

This next one happened to me again just a month or so ago. Well not the part about reuniting with my husband, but....I got up, showered, and then ran out to do my morning errands. It included the grocery store and post office. Since it was local, I just wore some athletic type pants. When I got home, I looked down and noticed the bright blue seams going down either side of my leg plus the flapping tag in the back. I had done it again! Why in the world no one seems to think it's important to tap me on the shoulder and point it out is beyond me!

I now take my embarrassing moments seriously and currently practice safety goals: it's called breathe deeply and slow down!

However, some people and situations in life just cannot be taken seriously. Stay tuned for the odd people we have met.

Chapter 43: Seargent Rodick and Other Oddities

You had to see it to believe it. That is how Ron described a Seargent (Sgt.) in the Air Force who was his higher up and the person to whom he reported. Sgt. Rodick marched to the beat of his own drum. Or more accurately the thrum of his bicycle pedals. In fact, I really did not believe it until I met him.

When we were stationed in rural England it was commonplace to have dripping rain, fog, and crazy drivers flying down single track (one lane) country roads. We considered the practice of riding bicycles on a single track road in the fog something we would not embark on. Sgt. Rodick, however, fully embraced it. He was fearless! Ron routinely witnessed Sgt. Rodick biking up to the base entrance on his way to work and always on time! He had the route down to a science and appeared to be oblivious to any dangers. His trek was a good 10 miles which added to the odds for an accident.

One day when Ron approached the Air Force base gate, he viewed Sgt. Rodick in an old battered English car: the ones where the steering wheel is located on the right side of the car. He noticed him simply because the Sgt. rarely drove the old vehicle and it was not at his usual time: he was late. It was a standing joke that only he would drive such a beat up car and still push it to 90 mph. On the rare occasion the Sgt. drove onto base he was alone: no one was brave enough to ride shotgun.

When Ron joined him in their building, Sgt. Rodick was stomping back and forth muttering to himself. Above his right eyebrow and on the right side of his face were discolored spots with a small gash. The troops in the room exchanged puzzled looks as if to say *I know he's strange but this is unusual even for him.* Unable to stand the suspense, Ron interrupted his little rant and asked the obvious questions: *was there something wrong; what had happened?*

Much to the delight of everyone in the room, while taxing their ability to mask the hilarity of the situation, Sgt. Rodick described the event that happened on his attempt to bicycle into work that morning. He was progressing quite nicely in spite of the fog. Suddenly out of nowhere a huge bird flew into his face! The impact was so solid that the bird died on contact. He said that he could feel the warm blood of the bird oozing down his skin. A citizen nearly ran over him as he lay bewildered on the side of the road, still trying to grasp what had happened. The bird was lying about 5 feet away from where he had swiped it off his face. (I was ready to hurl while hearing this story: I honestly don't know how the Sgt. didn't lose it; well ok, maybe he did.) It reminded me of an event that happened quite a while ago when the male model, Fabio, had a bird fly into his handsome face when he was riding a roller coaster. Of course the paparazzi got a hold of a picture with the whole bloody mess.

As for Sgt. Rodick, the driver passing by offered to take him and his slightly mangled bicycle home. Not deterred, Sgt. Rodick cleaned up and made his way straight to work. Ron and the other troops were nearly beside themselves as he recounted the story: a hundred one liners running in and out of their minds. Happily, a Major happened to be in the room and with no fear of rank loudly declared what they were all thinking. Ron said you could have heard a pin drop as they watched him struggle for composure.

You would think that this event would have deterred the Sgt. from bicycling again in the fog but that was not to be the case. In fact, he liked biking long distances so much that he mounted an ashtray to the rear fender of his bike. I kid you not; his smoking habit would not allow him to go an extended period of time without a smoke so he would light up while pedaling, never missing a beat. You're probably wondering why he didn't just flick his ashes on the damp ground but for whatever reason he insisted on using that ashtray! How he managed to twist, flick, and remain upright is a mystery to me! We finally concluded that Sgt. Rodick enjoyed making people ill at ease and being the source of much amusement. On top of everything else he fancied himself to be a ladies man: really? Do you have a Sgt. Rodick in your life?

Do you ever have people you do not know intimately begin dropping names in their conversation with you? They ramble on as if you've known each other for years while you're not following a word because you're still trying to figure out whom Kylie or Dirk is. For me, I always ask, "and who is that?"

It never ceases to amaze me when they answer in a strong almost offended tone that practically screams *it's so and so dumbshit!"*

What about people who just like to hear themselves speak? Do they not know how odd it makes them not to mention annoying?

At one point in my life I worked for 9-1-1 emergency services. If you want odd, get a job there. The calls ranged from horrible emergencies to psyche patients just wanting to report their latest hallucination. We had a former high school English teacher who used to call like clockwork: she was always hearing noises and the noises would become voices and they were always out to get her. Fortunately for her she had a son who was a lawyer. The city had to sue her because she was tying up the lines with 60 calls per minute. As soon as the call was disengaged she would call back. I honestly felt sorry for her because I understood that her mental illness was very real and she wasn't dialed in. (Yes, I know it's a pun: there's one in the next paragraph, too: I can't help myself!)

Add to those calls our daily sodomy call. This lady was always being sodomized by microwaves. (I know: I can't explain it either). The microwaves could *range* from an oven to anything metal: even tinfoil. According to her the microwaves could be bounced from anything and they were always aimed her way.

Or what about our 8:00 am heart attack calls? It was so sad but also enormously embarrassing for the callers. It was not uncommon for the couple to be having morning sex and the spouse dying while on top of his spouse. The part that was odd to us was that these couples were elderly: we could not comprehend old people having sex! Shame on us! We'll all be old someday and then the truth will be known!

We had callers who were handcuffed to the toilet tank, had razor blades stuck in their teeth or steak knives in their eyes. We even had a guy who had used a potato peeler who proceeded to peel off the skin on his member. Evidently the hallucinogenic drugs convinced him it was just a nice big carrot ready to pare. I sincerely hope he did not go on to be a chef!

I've heard the callers calling 9-1-1 for directory assistance or for directions on their road trip. They do not think that their requests are odd for an emergency line at all.

I have met people who are the blackmailers: they put you in a difficult situation by setting you up with a witness in the room: someone who would be emotionally disappointed if you said no. Those people hit my odd list because it's not normal to me to use emotional blackmail. I guess that sounds naïve, doesn't it?

Perhaps after reading this far into the book you may think I'm one of those odd people. Or maybe I'm just being very real with you in this book. Real people can be relatable people.

In conclusion, no matter who you are, there is a Sgt. Rodick, a rambler, or eccentric person you have encountered. One such eccentric person was King Xerxes. Like us, he suffered from insomnia. In the next chapter, we'll consider what lengths we go to in order to welcome sleep!

Chapter 44: The Lengths We Go To

King Xerxes reigned in 127 provinces from 486-465 B.C. The provinces were from India to Ethiopia. You can imagine what a busy person he must have been. Additionally, he had knee-jerk reactions; I wonder if he often laid in bed at night thinking *maybe I shouldn't have said I'd give you half the kingdom*.....I mention him because history actually records he had trouble sleeping one night. His resolution was to have an attendant read to him from the book of the history of his reign. (And you thought THIS book was boring).

When I considered this, I realized we have not discussed if there are physical reasons we do not fall asleep. Since you are reading this book, reading is one of the items you do to dismiss the day's ruminations and replace them with subdued thoughts.

I sat (yes awake in bed) and began listing what it is I do in order to fall asleep. In chapter 34 I listed what may be keeping us awake from a psychological point of view and gave practical exercises to use that may calm mostly the anxious thoughts. I think this is a good time to remind ourselves of those lists and explore a bit farther.

Going back to the story of King Xerxes, one thing is patently clear. He was impulsive! There are several stories where he's throwing banquets to demonstrate his wealth and generosity. When he got deeper into his cups and something pleased him, he would make promises he couldn't keep. Speculate with me; if you speak too quickly, do you lay in bed at night with regret? Do you think about the coulda woulda shouldas? That could be what was going through King Xerxes mind as he wished for sleep.

There are all sorts of folklore shared about famous people who had the same problem: sleep eluded them. The reasons may have varied, but their journey to find a solution did not. Many of these people were authors. Let me tell you, authors have busy minds. They are always creating and when the stillness of night creeps in, their minds get even busier.

I have heard of insomniacs trying tangible things such as; going for solitary moonlit walks, opening windows for fresh air, hiring someone to hold their hand once in bed, having a pillow that hugs them, splashing Cognac in their milk (President Theodore Roosevelt), emulating the sound of rain, and all manner of food concoctions such as sardine and onion on rye. Bleck!

We did cover what goes on in the mind, but what about the body? This is not a scientific discussion whatsoever, only the ideas that come to me while I contemplate what goes wrong! And to play devil's advocate, some may say that nothing goes wrong at all: nighttime is simply when they are the most productive!

I experience restless legs. It's nearly impossible to describe it. I have heard some people say it feels like thousands of little bugs crawling up and down the back of their legs, while others say they have a lot of leg movement. For me, I have the feeling that I want to stretch my legs, in particular my hamstrings. The downside is that when I succumb to the stretching, as soon as I stop, the sensation returns. Some of you may have physicians who prescribe medication for this.

If you happen to be like me and hyper-sensitive to medication, you may find yourself seeking out alternatives. I try hot baths, begging my husband for a leg massage, or using a heating pad. Those seem to work the best for me: or a microwave heat pack placed at the area of sensitivity.

Others of you may have headaches. Some people claim that they get a wave of heat that flushes over their body and that once it strikes, they know it's all over: sleep is not going to come. And no, I am not talking about HOT FLASHES! Although.......

Along those same lines, I have heard about people who equally will experience a wave of nausea: almost a feeling of doom. Again, not scientific, but I do recall hearing someone say that in the world of Neurology, the feeling of doom can be a form of a seizure. Take it for what it's worth, but instead of assuming your sleep deprivation is psychological, consider that it may be physical.

I can almost see you rolling your eyes right now. You've complained to your physician repeatedly and you get the old *alleviate stress from your life lecture.* Patients sometimes feel that if a physician cannot cure them that they are slotted into the *stress* column. If you're really lucky, you'll have a proactive physician who may refer you out for a sleep study. Sleep studies can monitor your breathing habits, oxygen levels, heart rate, and eye and body movements.

There could be underlying psychological reasons beyond anxiety such as bipolar type II disorder where the brain cycles between manic levels (high energy, little sleep) to depressive states (low energy and sluggish). I don't really know, but what I do understand is this: being an insomniac is nothing to be ashamed of. The My Healthy Newsletter states that the clinical definition of insomnia says people feel impaired by the lack of sleep and then experience anxiety about it. The study doesn't include other diagnoses such as mental disorders or other medical conditions. That lands about 6% of people in that first category not considering the medical conditions. The definition almost doesn't make sense.

However, the percentage of people with sleep disruption is much broader. I have heard news stories reporting that about 25% of Americans complain of sleep disturbances. Maybe that will put it in perspective. My insomnia is not unique. And you know what else? I find myself envying those who say they have no problem sleeping; they can sleep anywhere. They try to find empathy on the rare occasion that they cannot sleep. Empathy is not forthcoming, though, because they simply have not experienced it to our degree, so therefore do not possess any data to fully compute what we are suffering.

So, if it's simply a busy mind, consider the lists in chapter 34. If you feel your insomnia goes deeper, explore your options and give yourself the freedom to research it and seek resolution.

Or, if you're like me, try all the above and then come to the conclusion. My name is _____ and I am an insomniac! Welcome!

Chapter 45. How to Remove Chapstick from the Dryer

There is no other place (I'm betting) where you will find step by step instructions regarding removing a tube of cherry Chapstick from your dryer.

A cautionary tale comes with this chapter as well as a moral to the story. See if you can find it.

Cherry Chapstick: maybe you've all tried this particular flavor of the waxy balm intended to coat ones' lips and soothe chapped dry lips. It is easily recognizable with a white cap, white twist at the bottom and Alizarin crimson color to the tube. It is about 2 inches in length allowing it to easily be slipped into your pocket or purse.

Some people are addicted to Chapstick. It is a product where once used on a routine basis, a need is developed. As a result, many Chapstick users collect several tubes. They will have one in the center console of their car, a glove box, cosmetic case, inside purse compartment, jacket pocket, pants pocket, backpack, bedside table, bathroom vanity drawer, suitcase pocket, laptop bag, shirt pocket; in fact, anywhere that little tube can be slipped and easily accessed you may find one. I wouldn't be surprised to find one buried in someone's backyard time capsule or emergency shelter. You Chapstick lovers simply cannot be without it.

All that said, no matter how much you need your Chapstick, I doubt you would willingly retain it within the confines of your dryer. Yet this is the dilemma my friend found himself in. (Right now you are probably thinking that given the places we can keep our Chapstick, it is not outside the realm of possibility that a tube of Chapstick would be found in the dryer.) Chapstick kept in pockets could easily be forgotten along with spare change (have you seen the jar I've nearly filled in my laundry room?) You insomniacs may have already gone off on tangents from that last sentence. You are mentally listing the other items left in pockets that I have not mentioned. Stop that!!!! Focus on the Chapstick!

What if your Chapstick didn't fall out of your pants pocket? When you find something in a pocket while sorting laundry; where do you put it? Yes, absolutely, right on top of the dryer.

Here's the tricky part. Every dryer has a place for excess lint to be deposited while the clothes are spinning around enjoying the hot air circulating around them. This is my layman's understanding here, but lint is thrust out from the clothes floating around until some sort of device attracts it and separates it.

How does the lint separate and float? When clothes are washed, the fabrics break down; in particular when the laundry is agitating; it's that motion which shakes up the clothes and swirls the dirt out of the fabric into the water. Pieces of cloth break off during this process. They are lighter than the intact fabric and can easily separate. When placed in a dryer, these separated pieces can fit through the holes in the wall of the dryer. I believe the holes are there so that the forced air can reach the clothes and circulate around them. The little pieces of clothing or lint can squeeze through these holes. Something must capture them which is why dryers have a screen to filter out the small particles thus preventing them from going through the vent hose and causing a possible blockage.

The vent hose is what most of you will think of as that accordion shaped aluminum or plastic cylindrical piece (about 6 inches in diameter) appended to the bottom rear of your dryer. The hot moist air pushes through that hose and to the outside. Sometimes the hose vents directly from the dryer if on an outside wall to the outdoors. If your dryer is located within interior walls, the vent pipe may snake below the floor boards and then outside.

Once the air begins to travel through the venting system, loose particles of clothing, or lint, are pushed along with it. Without a filter screen, lint would build up inside the back of the dryer and the venting hose thereby blocking the free movement of the air. The result would be a very humid laundry area because the moist air is backing back into your room and most importantly, a fire hazard.

Laundry lint is highly flammable. This is because many clothes are not flame-retardant. In fact, dryer lint is an item some people use as kindling to start fires. I do not recommend you try that without a fire expert. The lint screen should be changed after each load to prevent the backup of hot air for each load of laundry dried. Your unit will run more efficiently because the air is flowing more consistently and your clothes will dry faster.

All of this said, we now return to the subject of Chapstick. Our friend's lint catcher trap was located on the top of the dryer. It is about 9 inches wide and 18 inches in length. It slides in and out of the dryer barrel kind of like a rounded drawer. When it is drawn out, lint is attached to it. Some dryers have the lint trap just inside the unit on the lower portion opposite where you open the door. Those dryers are more likely to have Chapstick mishaps if the item was not removed from the offending pocket.

For those of you who place items on top of the dryer, i.e. Chapstick, and the lint filter is located on the exterior top portion of your unit, beware! Since Chapstick is a cylindrical item, it rolls. Unless your dryer is perfectly calibrated and things do not roll, you will be interested in this tale. Our friend, we'll call him Chris, removed his spare Chapstick from his pocket and placed it on top of his dryer. Now he normally does not clean lint after each drying, so when he pulls that lint drawer out, it is overflowing. So much so, that when he peeled the blanket of lint off, his hand bumped the Chapstick and sent it rolling into the now open drawer. The Chapstick plunked all the way down that drawer and lodged in the bottom of the dryer between the barrel and the outer back cover.

At this point you may be thinking, *so, big deal, it fell back there; come on, seriously?* This is where your insomnia will come in handy. You lay in bed and your brain surfs, right? You think about all manner of things. For example upon reading the title of this chapter you thought, *Chapstick, dry lips, man I'm thirsty, a cold beer is so good after cutting the grass, oh the grass is really long, I need to cut it tomorrow but when? I'm so busy at work, oh shoot, work. I've got to get that task completed before 9am or my boss will be riding my tail. My dog's tail wags so much I may have to amputate it. I feel inspired when I see amputees continuing their passion without a hitch. I really admire those people who do not consider themselves handicapped whatsoever and fly down mountains in their skis: it is really something! When I'm out in the elements like that, all I want is my Chapstick.*

See how that works? Use your same skills with what can happen when your Chapstick tube is residing in the bottom backside of your dryer. Surf through the potential consequences. Chapstick is made of a waxy substance. Wax is what candles are made of: could it melt back there and light up? Hmm, would it smell good, like cherries? I digress. What about the fact that located at the rear of your dryer is a fan that rotates while blowing the hot air out from the heating element? If you are my friend, Chris, you may have the misfortune for that tube to lodge right between the fan blades. If you concluded that it

328

suddenly lost its momentum and will not roll away from the fan, you are correct! What to do?

First of all, if you want to save money, phone a friend. Get yourself a screwdriver either flathead or Phillips (the star-shaped tip) depending on what type of screws are on the back of your unit. Tip your dryer forward while one person stands in front of it and balances it at about a 45-90 degree angle. Have the other person step behind the dryer after carefully separating the vent box or hose from the back of the dryer. (This is done by pulling it off after loosening typically what amounts to a clamp or twist tie of some sort).

The person in front of the dryer should hand off the screw driver to the person behind, much as a scrub nurse would hand over the scalpel on command of the surgeon. Back person must unscrew all the screws holding the metal back to the dryer which hides the inner mechanisms of the unit. Pull it off and set aside. If the helper at the front of the dryer is still propping it up, they could lay the dryer face down onto the floor while being careful to protect the door at the front so that it is not dented.

Once the back is removed, you can easily spot the Chapstick tube, reach your hand in, and retrieve the cylindrical offender. You probably should have the dryer unplugged if it's electric just in case the fan decided it wanted to work right then. (Remember, it could be that the *on* button would be depressed if the dryer is laying front side down.) When the Chapstick is safely out of the way, reverse the steps and reattach the metal (fireproof) back to the dryer, have your friend prop it back to its 45 degree angle, clamp the vent box or hose back to the unit making sure you have a tight seal to the hose system. At this time, make sure there is room for the person behind the dryer to exit (trust me, they can easily be trapped back there and the machinations necessary to remove them can be quite humorous). When they are out, gently upright the dryer and scoot into its original position, careful not to squeeze the vent hose too tightly to the wall.

This story had more than one moral to it. There are at least 4. See if you can think of what they are. If that is too taxing; go to sleep!

Chapter 46. Pet Peeves

Oh boy, we all have them; pet peeves! If I asked you to list them, my bet is that we'd find we are in agreement on some of them and then others, well, they are 100% subjective.

Sometimes we just need to vent, right? (I still have dryer vents on my mind.) It helps release the pressure, so here we go; my list!

Inside Out Laundry-Drives me nuts! Why do I have to pull that stupid shirt out of the dryer and turn it right side out before I hang it up? And yes, I no longer do it. If it goes into the laundry inside out, then it is washed, dried, and hung up the same way. Maybe you know my family? They're the ones with their collars always curled in?

Trail of Laundry-Routinely I throw up my hands in frustration. Over the weekend I took 2 of my husband's shirts that were lying on the bed and tossed them on the floor. They stayed that way 3 days until I relented. Then I went into his office where he does his homework and stuffed at the bottom of the office chair were 2 more shirts! Note….there was a clothes basket literally 2 feet from his shirts in the bedroom and a hamper 1 foot away from that!

Little Black Hairs-They sure do stand out against a white tile floor. Either the shedder should scrupulously clean them up after each shower or get a dark floor. I'm a realist: the floor color needs to change!

Repeating Myself-If you want to stop communication with me; ask me to repeat myself. It is not unheard of for me to just say "never mind" even if it was kind of important.

Redundancy-This is not the same as repeating myself. I'm talking about things like "Oh, that was super-duper cool!" "It was large and so big!" (You keep putting your mind in the gutter; pull it out!) "I heard the craziest kooky thing". "It was loud and amplified". "Turn right (north)". I'm trying to think of these as I go and meanwhile you are probably thinking of super-duper good ones. "Eliminate and end world hunger". "Run and Race 5-K Race". "For customer service, say *customer service*". "We vary in our different opinions that are subjective."

To sum redundancy up, I will quote my favorite bumper sticker; "Wipe out and Abolish Redundancy!" Enough Said!

Grocery Carts –I mean come on, the return rack is right next to them half the time. I park right next to the cart return rack: I figure it ups my odds that maybe one found its way into the rack.

Blinkers- This should probably go at the top of my list. It drives me craaaaazy! I detest sitting at a position in traffic where I could have proceeded had I known the car across from me was actually going to turn. Or, had I trusted the blinkers, I would have t-boned more cars than I can count. This does not give me license for road-rage, for the record.

Cell phones and drivers-One word: Distracted!

Cell phones and the loud talker-It's personal folks: I don't want to know what you did last night and with whom. And why when you're in a restaurant does your normal conversational tone of voice rise up at least 10 decibels when you answer your phone?

Worse of all are those of you who plant yourselves in a public toilet stall to hold a conversation. Do I really want to flush while seated in the stall next to you? Your caller gets to hear that. And, I'm a captive audience and I don't want to be captivated by your conversation!

Cell Phones at Inappropriate times- If you are in a scheduled meeting, out to dinner, on a date, being intimate; do NOT answer your cell phone if it's not an emergency.

Farting on an airplane-Remember Chapter 17? Well, it's just downright wrong! And I hold that opinion for selfish reasons: I'm afraid someone will think that it's me.

Pregnancy Stories (sorry moms to be)-It's like the Moms are swapping war stories, which in their minds is probably what it was like; but it's a battle most people in your audience have fought as well. Each Mom glazes over as they hear the details of labor pains, how far apart, if their water broke, how much weight they gained, how many hours and seconds each lasted, epidural or no epidural, cesarean section pros and cons, if they had a coach, benefits of natural deliveries, how many people in a room, how hungry they were, how grumpy they were, how many people they punched out while in phase 3 and and and…..you know what happens next. Moms 2, 3, 4, and 5 are not to be outdone so their stories are added.

They threw up for the first 5 months; but wait, Mom 4 never threw up at all she exclaims with a superior self-satisfied (redundancy, see?) smile. This brings me to my next pet peeve.

One-sided Conversations-This sends one message: "I don't care about you, I care about numero Uno, and anything you contribute to this conversation is of no consequence." Literally, if I try to inject an observation into the one-sider's monologue, they will jump right over my words as if I never uttered them. I am not about to repeat myself.

And, if you are generous and give them another shot at being a good listener while you try to slip in your own phrase, you can become disillusioned. Much to your chagrin the one-sider gives you a glazed nod and then without missing a beat picks up right where they left off. And why in the world are they gifted with such a specific memory where they can give you a minute by minute replay of whatever topic they have warmed up to? It's incredible, really. They are special and they know it.

Their, There, They're- So here it is. *"Their"* - It shows possession. "Their shoe, their house, their ideas".

"There"- A noun; a place. "Look over there at the pond". "There it is."

"They're" - A contraction: two words put together; specifically "they are". If you cannot say they are in place of "they're" then you have the wrong word.

Your, You're- *Your* shows possession. "Your side of the bed." Your book, your right, your idea; all yours!"

You're-Another contraction and no I'm not speaking about your childbirth stories. It is *you are* put together so use the same logic as with *they're.*

Gossiping; the Whisperer-In my opinion, if you are in the presence of people other than the one to whom you are speaking, you are not in a movie theater or restaurant, it is not a surprise for someone, and you are in an area where voices are not subdued, then you do not need to whisper. Whisperers smack of being gossipers. If you have to whisper it, then do not say it. For all of you who are jumping up, mentally yelling "yes but...." Reread my qualifying opening sentence. This is in the context of environments where it is acceptable to have a normal level of volume such as the proverbial office water cooler, a break room, the foyer of a building, etc.

Perfect Parents-I'm not a perfect parent so it rubs me the wrong way when I see people whose children have no faults, who never lose their temper and put on a pretty face no matter what the life situation is. Sometimes parenting is hard and we know it, yet the perfect people's lives are coming up roses! Unrelatable!

Perfect Partners-Your partner is perfect? You never fight? I have nothing to say!

Poor Customer Service- This is a big one for me! My number one customer service pet peeve is when I'm ignored; particularly in a medical office. I do not want to be there in the first place, so when I approach the front desk personnel and I am completely ignored, I get uncomfortable. Do I simply sit down, scan the counter for a sheet to sign while writing my name in huge letters so they can't miss it, or do I clear my throat try to make eye contact and keep a smile plastered on my face? Why can't they raise one finger, give me a nod and let me know I'm visible?

Or what about the hated "ring bell for service". I have a good example from today. I went to the post office where a man came out and held the door open for me after entering a couple seconds before. I thought, "wow, he thinks I'm attractive and came back out to try a maneuver: but I'm married, so..." And then I see he has a nametag but I don't catch what it says. I approach the lobby window as he goes into some side door, evidently a post office employee. I don't see anyone around other than one woman filling out a change of address card. In the front is a sign that says "ring bell for service". Right when I'm thinking I'll have to make that hated noise and draw attention to myself, the door opener guy steps up to the encounter with "may I help you?" I was so thankful to be acknowledged before I rang that bell. Somehow I felt I was to divine that the door holder was the person who would assist me and that I was to wait. And confirmation: he was NOT attracted to me. I know that probably didn't make any sense: but basically, I hate ringing bells.

Whiners –I have complete empathy for those who suffer from depressive tendencies. I am not referring to physical conditions; I am talking about the people who see the glass half empty. It's not even the viewpoint that gets me; it is the tone in their voices. It just sounds like complaining. It's the gnawing wah wah wah tonal quality to their voice. I don't mind someone complaining or sharing but whining is annoying.

People who Sound like They're Asking a Question at the End of a Sentence? - It seems as if more and more conversations have a person who ends a statement with a rise in inflection at the end of their sentences. Such as "I'm going to the movies on Friday?" "I'm a good singer and I wanted to sing this song?"

Multiple syllables for a one syllable word.- I have always joked that I never saw so many syllables in one 3-lettered word than. "Mooooooooommmmm" !!!! The newest one I hear a lot is: instead of yes or yeah it has an "ah" on the end. Yes-ah, or yeah-ah. "That was amazing-gah" And my personal most hated. "No-ah". I realize I sound like a grump but if you think about it, we all have our fingernails down the chalkboard moments.

Smart Phone auto-correct-Oh boy can that one get us into trouble, not to mention make us look ignorant! I think they're hilarious until it's my text or email that goes out. Then it annoys me! I know, I'm a perfectionist and they're annoying, too!

Dreams I can't Remember- Even when I lay in bed thinking I'll remember this one, because I'm not really sleeping that deeply; poof-it evaporates into thin air!

Phantom Thermostat Resetters- In the work place. "I'm freezing". "It's roasting". And the temp gods must observe the thermostat, take note of people's built-in thermostats and then find the neutral sacred ground. Notes are put on the thermostat saying "do not change thermostat", company emails sent out outlining the policy, yet mysteriously these pre-programmed thermostats have a life of their own. The "freezers" are suspiciously satisfied while the "heaters" are loudly complaining. I think world wars could be started over room temperatures.

Food Smackers- This one doesn't really bother me so much, but my daughter would disown me if I didn't give it a nod. I will go one step further, though, and say that I don't want to see the partially chewed food while you are masticating it.

People Who Sleep! - I think we all agree on this one.

Obnoxious People –You know the type; they must hold court, are loud, talk incessantly, snore, belch, fart, cough to get your attention, return their food at the restaurant, make really particular meal orders, drive too fast, cut off other drivers, blare their music with their windows down at a stoplight and pretty much encompass a lot of my pet peeves all bundled into one obnoxious person! But do you know what drives me over the top more than any other pet peeve? Mean People!

Chapter 47. Mean People

When mean people unjustly dole out their nastiness, I find myself lying awake chewing on the injustice of it all! Do you ever reflect about all of the things you could have said? It's an exercise in frustration.

We all have different opinions about what consists of a mean person. The view we all share is that they are not fair and we should have handled them differently.

We insomniacs tend to cure all that ails the world while we lay in bed with eyes wide open. Encountering mean people reminds us of what it is that is wrong with society.

When I come up empty, I'll train the microscope on myself; replaying the event over and over on a continuous loop until I can find something that may have triggered the treatment I received. I ask myself all sorts of questions; maybe you do, too, such as:

- Did I roll my eyes?
- Am I unreasonable?

- Did I interrupt?

- Do I look grumpy?

- Is there a phrase tattooed across my forehead declaring "abuse me"?

- Am I too nice and thus earning the disdain from the mean person?

- Is it the way I was dressed?

- Did they read the uncharitable thoughts in my mind?

- Were those thoughts reflected on my face?

- Do I smell or something?

- Am I just too good looking and intimidating? (I quickly shake that one off and make myself laugh in spite of my ire: right up there with they hate skinny people).

- Was I too cheerful and they didn't buy it?

- They hate morning people?

- Maybe I took a deep breath before responding which made me look exasperated?

- Or perhaps it was that sigh that escaped.......

- Do I seem insincere, proud, or arrogant?

- If I had given them a bright smile would it have stopped them?

Now that my painful self -analysis is over, I begin thinking about the person who is driving me crazy. I'll find myself lying there trying to turn the other cheek (pun); finding some sort of insight that will allow me to understand why they act the way they do.

- Did they have a bad day?

- Are they normally a negative person?

- Were they suffering neglect at someone else's hands and paying it forward to me?

- Did someone forget to thank them for something they did?

- Are they money hungry?

- Maybe they're very insecure and posturing.

- Maybe they had a life changing event that recently occurred.

- Secretly, they are mad at themselves, not me.

- Was there some sort of gossip on my part that they heard about? (I wrack my brain trying to think if I have anything to be guilty of and breathe a sigh of relief when I realize I'm innocent).

- Maybe they're just a sarcastic person and I'm being overly sensitive.

Now that I've gone through all of those steps and find myself still awake I realize I must give in and allow myself to be angry. Anger can be healthy when it's released in the right way. I view it as righteous indignation! If I didn't deserve it and I can't find a reason why they dished out the negative vibes, then I have the right to be angry! And, even if I did deserve it, it doesn't excuse them to stooping to such a low level. (Can you feel my ire building even as I write this?)

So, we all agree; we're angry. Now how do we take that emotion and direct it to the offender? Disclaimer here: in no way shape or form do I support violence, although I'm sure we've all had those uncharitable fantasies at one point or the other.

If it is somebody I'm not likely to encounter again, I let myself rant and rave while I replay the offense in my mind.

If the mean person is someone that is not a friend, but one I expect to run into again (maybe in a place of business), then I will contemplate confronting them. I ask myself if I'll express my disdain for what they did to me or if I'll be passive aggressive. A good example of this would be a person in customer service; restaurants come to mind.

I'm typically very polite to wait staff even when they are distracted. Many of us have some special something we add to our order. Mine is I detest butter so I will ask that my hamburger bun or my pancakes do not have butter on them: I stress it with an apologetic smile. For the record, they rarely get it right because it's evidently a very alien request. A couple weeks ago I went to a pancake type restaurant chain. I stressed no butter please on my pancakes. (Ugh, disgusting). When the waitress brought my pancakes there was a generous scoop of butter right in the middle of the top pancake. I explained that I requested no butter and to be fair I said if they could just replace the top pancake that was fine; I didn't want to be a hassle. Now waitresses need their tips and many times it is not really their fault, so this one was quick to apologize and take it back to the kitchen. What she didn't know was that I could hear everything being said in the kitchen. Our waitress told the manager that the guest requested no butter and seemed to be giving an explanation to her boss as to why she would waste a pancake. When I heard the manager tell her, "scrape the butter off and flip the pancake over; she'll never know", I was livid! Yet, when the young embarrassed waitress came back out of the kitchen after an appropriate amount of time, I smiled at her. I felt that it wasn't her fault but inside I was fighting mad.

Am I the only wimp here? I can almost hear some of you declaring that you would have asked for the manager right then and there. Yet I was in a dilemma. We live in a smaller town: I'm a potential return customer to that restaurant and I don't want them getting even with me on my next order. So I acted ignorant and when she walked away, calmly flipped over my pancake, saw the wet spot in the middle and put it to the side. Maybe she saw it on the side and got the point.

Now here's the problem: guess what I did when I went to bed that night? I kicked myself from here to eternity for being such a pushover. I stewed over it and decided I must take action or else sleep was going to elude me the remainder of the night. I got out of bed, fired up my computer, found the restaurant review websites and told my story. I felt justified and satisfied that I did something. And, guess what? I'm not going back to that restaurant! It's one more little way I can repay the mean person: they lost my business.

You all have your experiences ranging from childhood bullying, unfair partners, to horrible bosses. Sometimes you're accused of something with no way to defend yourself in the moment because of potential backlash. It is unfair and makes you feel helpless. I am not a professional, but I am an insomniac and as one I say: allow yourself to be angry so that you can deal with it. Otherwise, the same issue will continue to haunt you. You need an outlet.

Maybe reading this chapter will at least let you know we all have encountered mean people and we all wish to deal with their behavior in a manner that is appropriate yet effective! I don't know about you, but unjust people really get under my skin! Our next chapter will be more light-hearted. After all,

even funny things can keep our thoughts active at
night.

Chapter 48. Auto Replay

My husband *thinks* he is the king of puns. I say he is the king of *bad* puns. Maybe that is why I have so many sprinkled into this book: he has rubbed off on me. The problem with him is that he can't resist an opportunity to throw one out there. It's almost like a tick; if someone or something provides the line, he has to pun it out. I can see it coming and I immediately say "oh no, you're going to blow; don't do it, don't do it". And he can no more hold it in than the man in the moon.

I find that people I'm around a lot influence me. As much as I hate to admit it, I find myself wanting to find the perfect pun to impress my husband. I tell myself it is his love language and it is: he becomes enormously proud and laughs way beyond what the pun was worth; he gets so tickled. When he makes a pun that I actually laugh at, he can't control his laughter: it is a belly laugh and he becomes even more proud of his humor.

If you like puns, too, then right now you may find yourself conjuring up come dorky ones as well.

What really gets me is that when someone puts out a straight line, I must make a joke about it.

And it is very frustrating when they take you seriously. I cannot tell you how many times I find myself saying "it's a joke, it's a joke" while I'm silently thinking, "you can't really think I'd be that stupid, can you?" Know your audience!

What about the catchy song? I'm sure advertising agencies are patting themselves on the back when they hear their commercial jingle being hummed in our nation's living rooms just as they had hoped. Every generation has one that immediately springs to mind and won't leave. Sometimes it is a practice of patience to wipe those little ditties from our minds. I know many people who hum the jingle but have no idea what the product is that corresponds with it.

If I hear a song later in the day, I end up playing it over and over in my mind when I go to bed. It is ridiculous! I try to deal with it by reciting another one. The problem occurs when it's another catchy song. I'm caught in a continuous loop of nocturnal crooning.

Have you ever been at work or some other function and found that you said something profound? Everyone around you was either laughing or earnestly nodding their heads, leaning in toward you, one hundred percent engaged? And then when you come home and things quiet down for the night, you find yourself recalling the conversation? I will even find I silently chuckle to myself, giving the self-congratulatory slap on the back. But, as often happens when I try to replay my amazing wit, I can't remember exactly what I had to say. In fact, all I can remember is that I definitely said something great because of the way the people around me reacted. I think and think yet I can't come up with it. I'll end up deciding that I was good and find myself in awe that I even came up with the quip in the first place, since if you asked me to be that artful at that moment, I would be inept.

The other night I was in the middle of a competitive game night when one of the participants made a statement where I had to literally stop the timer, share the one-liner and watch the room erupt in laughter. It may be hard to give you the visual, but about right now maybe a good laugh would be just the ticket. It was this: My 4 year old niece was bouncing around the room during our game on a rubber ball with a handle. She was seated on it and I'd say it was probably larger than a basketball but smaller than a Pilates ball. We were pretty much all ignoring her until my uncle Gary said: "That is what happens when you swallow your chewing gum". I'm still laughing as I write this. Do you ever do that? You hear something, have to wait a beat for it to sink in and then just die laughing? That's how this was. Once he made that comment, although not a pun, my husband's estimation of him moved up 10 notches. And yes, the challenge was on; how could we top that?

What about arguments with someone close to you? Are you a grudge holder or are you like me? I know I was angry, but I can't remember why. I'm sure the people involved in disagreements with us forgetfuls are relieved, but it doesn't change the fact we were angry. Absolutely, I will lie down at night and try to recall what in the world it was that drove me nuts in the first place. I find myself getting agitated when the next fight comes up and I'm fairly certain this is a topic from a previous discussion, yet I can't recall it. At that point, I want to childishly stomp my foot because I know I will not be able to use that to prove my point. Now if you ascribe to the belief (as I actually do) that you should not let the sun go down on your anger, then this is an exercise you shouldn't do in the first place. If you're still chewing on your anger at bedtime, then it must not have been dealt with to your satisfaction. I react to verbal fights the way I do to jokes: I hear a funny joke, but I am unable to repeat it: if I try the first part, then I forget the punch line, or I give the punch line but forget the setup.

Another way to experience auto-replay is long term memory. Short term memory is trickier: I find that many people can recall events long ago much more rapidly than short term. This contradicts the previous paragraph but let me explain. If the situation does not directly affect me, then for some silly reason, I can recall it. And again, I'm going to contradict myself, because if it is something that really interests me, I can remember. For example: I always remember what I was wearing for anything that was significant enough for me to recall in the first place. I have been told we remember what we find important. Confusing; I know! Do you feel as if I just took you in a big circle?

For those of us who enjoy observing other people, we find that our computer brains file the information away. We can remember what hair style someone had from ten years ago, but we can't recall the last movie we saw. I seem to memorize random pieces of information about almost anyone I encounter and it generally blows their mind when I mention it years later. This is where our brains are so cool! Sometimes auto-replay is a great thing.

Auto-replay is also very useful for television. Our remotes are awesome! We can rewind, jump back, bump forward, and never miss a beat. If you don't understand what the actor said, you just go back 30 seconds. When I worked at 9-1-1, we could replay the recording of the call in case there was something we needed to clarify.

I often wish that I could bump back conversations, rewind the radio in the car when I hear something I love, or fast forward a boring conversation. Remotes would enhance every area of my life. I comfort myself with the fact that if I had a remote, than I wouldn't really listen to the person speaking to me and that would make me a bad friend, listener, or neighbor.

Last, when I can't rely on my brain or a physical recording device, I write it down! From what I hear, writing isn't 100% out yet. We don't have every single thing on One Note, Word, our e-calendars, and Smart phones. They still sell paper and pens and sometimes the old fashioned way is convenient for recalling those things we do remember. I don't have a pretty segue way into the next chapter but this one is closed!

Chapter 49. Changing Geographic Locations

Think of one word to describe you. Mine is *Wanderlust.* Your word might be; *boring, energetic, gregarious, conservative, secure, liberal, adventurous, cautious, successful, controversial, sarcastic, stuck and on....*

Consider this: moving for the sake of a new adventure. That is what we do! Whenever we change locations, it is always with a sense of awe at the differences in the culture.

I moved to the Midwest after spending most of my life in other places; most notably the Southwest. Since returning, I have been in culture shock.

People out here are quite simply; open. It was as if the welcome wagon was waiting when we moved here and the hearts and doors of the new neighborhood were open both figuratively and literally. It can be overwhelming when you are accustomed to areas where people have fences and are more reticent. Now these people don't walk you through life here, they're just willing to make friendships and do not comprehend there may be social differences.

I discovered people gather for something called "Trivia Night". A hall is rented, tables large enough to hold 8 people are placed around the room, and there are tables in the front of the room displaying various items to bid on during the silent auction.

Each game table cost $125 to "rent" and will hold 8-10 participants.

An MC (master of ceremonies or announcer) is selected, and pre-printed sheets loaded with trivia questions are distributed.

This is the part that gets weird to me. (Good weird, by the way). Participants will bring food; all kinds of food for their table. There will be spread of anything and everything for just their table. It can be crock pots full of soups and stews to movie popcorn and cookies.

The tables are given a pre-set amount of time and one sheet of questions: "ready, set, go". The MC has started the clock. If someone at your table has a bit of cash, they can purchase stickers and use one per sheet for an automatic correct answer on their sheet. The night proceeds in this manner, sheet after sheet, heads locked together, while tables mingle and bond. The stickers don't seem fair if you're competitive like me.

I forgot to mention that people also bring their troll dolls or Justin Bieber bobble heads for good luck and place them on the table. I'm told this is commonplace at Bingo halls. Drinks and food continue to flow and there is a general feeling of good will in the air. I had not ever experienced this in the desert southwest: maybe I didn't hang with the right crowd or maybe it's a geographical thing. One helpful hint for Trivia night: have a variety of ages at your table so that your experience is vaster.

What about listening to bands in folding chairs with your neighborhood friends at the parking lot of a local frozen custard shop? I'm not kidding: 300 people can turn up for their custard and music. This didn't happen in the desert: either your ice cream would melt or you would.

If you want more music, there's a symphony in the park, or open microphone at the uptown burger bar. If it is wintertime, then laser tag, bowling, game nights, and cooking for your friends is not uncommon. I also noticed the local YMCA is quite popular during inclement weather; it has an indoor track, heated pool, indoor tennis courts, rock climbing wall; anything a person could desire.

Now yard work is another thing. When we lived in the desert we had rock in the front and back yards instead of grass. Those who chose to have grass had to spend a lot of money monthly on their water bill. When they received their water bill it was enormous. And you could only water on assigned days in an effort by the cities to conserve water. A lot of people cheat on this so the water companies increase the charge when a certain usage is reached.

For us, yard work consisted of spraying the weeds that grow even in the desert, and raking the rocks to keep them uniform. We didn't own a lawnmower. When our dog pooped in the yard, it was a simple matter to scoop it up from the rocks. Poor dog; hot rocks and no cool grass.

There are plants to water that are hearty types that accept direct sunlight; a daily splash of water will generally do it. The rest are cacti and they do not require water. Now fast forward to moving to a place with climate changes. Consider what culture shock it is: there is no guide for how to care for Midwest yards. It requires research and asking questions. In order to research, I had to know which questions to ask: it was trial and error. I have found that if I ask 3 people 3 different questions, I get 3 different answers. I learned that I must observe the area and people around me.

There are leaves everywhere during the Fall. When I saw how many leaves were littering the yard and sidewalk, I felt action was required. I didn't want to get on the wrong side of the neighbors. So I got outside with what I was told was a leaf rake and began making piles. (Rock rakes are metal with short tines). I was a little perturbed that the other people in the area didn't have as many leaves. Much to my embarrassment MJ, the next door neighbor came out and asked me what I was doing. I must have looked at her as if she had two heads because I said, "raking leaves?" And do you know what she did? She laughed at me! "Nobody rakes leaves out here: just use a mulch blade and mow them". And yes, I didn't know what a mulch blade was! That was our first house.

Then we moved to a different area in the same town and when the trees began shedding, I noticed again that we had all the leaves. So I went outside to mow the lawn and mulch the leaves. Instead of making the situation better, it sprayed the leaves all over the sidewalk and street. I hear there is a thing called a leaf bag for the lawnmower and figured out I should have used that after I had blown mulched leaves everywhere.

In this older Midwest neighborhood, I learned there are people called *lawn genie* senior citizens. They are meticulous about their lawns, pulling every little weed, watering their flowers, and stooping to grab every single leaf. It looks painful watching them stoop yet they are hearty. Literally, a 91 year old lady was out in her yard today with a leaf blower; I thought I was hallucinating!

As luck would have it, one of these lawn genies kitty corner from our yard was across the street with a rake, pointedly looking at my house. The wind had kicked up and all the bits of leaves in the street were headed straight toward her yard. What a way to get off on the wrong foot with them!

So I asked myself; do people sweep leaves out of the street? I've heard of street sweeper machines but have never seen one here. I was afraid I looked ridiculous but I grabbed the push broom and began sweeping the leaves back toward the curb. Who, I wondered, literally swept the street? I knew it was a gamble: either I gained *lawn genie's admiration* or I looked like I was cuckoo for Cocoa Puffs. Then I fired up a leaf blower but was clueless how to use it. Somehow I managed to blow the leaves back up to the yard where I then began raking. I wanted to yell across the street to the *lawn genie* that I was new at this and to give me a break. The Welcome Wagon people do not leave fliers in their bag for us newbies explaining lawn etiquette. I still haven't figured out leaf etiquette as it is a subjective topic. My lesson that day was that not everyone is as warm and welcoming as I had thought. In fact, nothing against seniors, but I felt that they had earned their stripes and figured that I needed to earn mine, too. No advice was forthcoming. And maybe they resented out of towners.

We all have our loyalties to our sports teams. Ours lies firmly with our favorite college in the Pac 12; Arizona! (Go Wildcats!) Those of you outside of the Pac 12 are probably thinking I'm crazy for not rooting for *your* chosen teams. However, I admit, I do not do well at following professional football although I enjoy attending the college games in my old hometown. So in the spirit of embracing the teams in my area, I purchased a football shirt for the big NFL team here. It was muted and not overt.

Even that was a gaff. Evidently the fans here aren't as fanatical when their team isn't doing well. The comments I received were "why are you wearing that shirt? They're not any good; no one here really cares for them!" Ugh! So far I was losing at yard work brownie points and sports apparel. What was next?

Apparel was next: I learned that it rains here and even snows. Both of these elements are rare where I recently came from. Rain was a novelty in the Southwest: at work everyone would run outside to get wet. It was understood that Mother Nature's gift was an automatic break for all staff. At home, my husband and I would go outside into the monsoon rainstorms and let ourselves get soaked with arms uplifted. It was cleansing. Nobody thought it was strange. And then we came here......When it rained lightly without lightning and thunder we decided to go for a walk and enjoy it. People were literally driving by craning their necks as they passed us with expressions that said it all. It was either a neighbor rolling down their window asking if we needed a ride, or looks from strangers that seemed to say "are those people crazy?" Oh, and we don't own rain boots. We didn't realize people wore them for anything other than a fashion statement of some sort. The other items of apparel we still do not possess are waterproof jackets nor do we ever remember to carry an umbrella. When it rains, my cotton jackets or sweatshirts are soaked through. I still leave jackets in restaurants, because I am not accustomed to having them on my person in the first place.

And then comes winter. The balmy 70 degree days do not exist like they did in the Southwest. Each time it snowed here my husband and I would don our hiking boots and go for a walk. (No, we still do not own snow boots). We would have to gingerly pick our way over icy sidewalks or snow-covered walks. Before we would head out, our shovels would be out so that we could considerately clear the sidewalk for the other walkers. Did you know that the majority of the people do not shovel their sidewalks? Again, we got the crazy looks from people in the area for doing something as simple as shoveling.

Being in a new geographic location is like an alien landing from a distant planet. I am beginning to think I have green skin and an antennae protruding from my brain that says "different, different!"

If you were a military spouse like me, you had a military base with all sorts of resources and/or military families to explain the ropes to you. A sponsor was assigned. This sponsor would show you where to buy your groceries, explain where you had to take your local driving test (England was really fun!), popular places to eat, and names for produce that were different if we were out of the country. Many times there would be a meal waiting for us at our new place, warm and welcoming. I could give you an entire chapter on being new to a foreign country. Did you know the British think I have an accent? And, they thought it was French Canadian, yet I've never even been to Canada.

I have decided that there needs to be a relocation office in every town for new-comers to report. Each person or family should be assigned a sponsor who is there to answer all questions the new resident may have. I think it would eliminate so many of the embarrassing situations that can arise. No matter what, it is up to us as the new person in town. I have decided it is all about our attitudes and our choice to be happy!

Chapter 50. Happiness

Happiness was an elusive emotion for me much of my life. I floundered while fighting the slippery image I thought perhaps had been created exclusively for greeting card companies, and company morale boosters.

Forms of the word "happiness" are thrown around like pieces of cottony fluff to chase in flight. I would find myself running around trying to grasp onto it while trying not to let it slip through my fingers.

There are more definitions of happiness than I can name. I commonly hear the following floating around in conversations:

"I'm so happy: I'm in love!"

"Happy is as Happy Does" (Forrest Gump?)

"Happiness is a conscious decision", "money can't buy happiness, but it sure helps!"

"Happiness is elusive"

"Happiness is over-rated"

"I'm always happy" (puke)

"I thrive on attention: being in the center makes me happy"

"I'm happy when I can blend into the background: I like being a wallflower."

"A day at the spa makes me happy"

"Giving makes me happy"

"Having enough money to pay my bills"

"Helping others in need"

"Shopping, of course!"

"When I get a full nights' rest"

We could fill the pages of this book simply by providing our own lists. We all have a different yardstick to measure happiness by; it's subjective. To me it's condescending when someone tells you their point of view and believes it is the only one that will make you happy. When I get pissy, I remove myself from those people.

One day we may feel happy when "x" happens and another day nothing makes us happy. (Maybe you read the book "Be Joyful, it Beats Being Happy". Say what????)

If someone receives an accolade you think you were deserving of, you may politely say, "I'm so happy for you." as you grit your teeth between your tightly pursed lips. (A white lie or is it a downright fib?)

Perhaps you or someone you know suffers from depression and jokes about needing their "happy" pills. Since you're probably an insomniac if you're reading this book, you just might be on "happy pills" to help you sleep. You can decide whether or not that statement offends you.

Reading this back, you would think happiness was enough money, beauty, sayings no one can comprehend, better living through chemicals, or title ticklers to entice a reader.

Believe it or not, I think I do know what happiness is (for me). It is the gift of hindsight: a clear gaze back at what was and what could have been. Life situations where we thought happiness did not exist which were in actuality infused with happiness.

Both my daughter and my best friend happened to live in the same seedy apartment complex. Both were newly married, struggling to put their husbands through college, while living in cockroach infested apartments. They were horrified that each time a crumb was on their counter, a cockroach would run out, grab the crumb, and scurry back to its hiding place. To sum it up; they were grossed out!

The homeless slept outside by their dumpsters, and occasionally they would hear gunshots in the near distance. How in the world could couples newly engaged in marital bliss find happiness in this situation?

My words to them were that someday they would look back at those times as some of the happiest in their lives. The looks I received in return could have burned holes into my brain, but I persisted.

Now a decade later, they understand. Their life was simple back then. They have the circle completed. They all fully get it that sometimes the leaner days were the best days: they were less complicated.

They learned to have compassion for low income or no income people who were many times hungry and homeless and thankful for but a scrap of fresh food that may have been disposed of. The homeless were not concerned about cockroaches and crumbs. Survival was happiness for them. My daughter and friends didn't realize how happy it made those people when they gave one of them a lift to a soup kitchen, or brought a plate of leftovers out to them, or shared a coat they really didn't wear.

To be fair, happiness doesn't always have to be selfless. It's not a crime to enjoy the finer things in life. For those of you who have paid the price by pushing yourself through school, worked grueling hours, and experienced many sacrifices, you probably now feel great satisfaction seeing the fruits of your labor. On the opposite side of this spectrum, there are those of you who get stressed out by having the huge home and garage full of toys because they're one more thing you need to care for. Neither is wrong; it's what your definition of happiness is.

For me, happiness is formed by the simplest things in life. A shared look with my husband that only we understand, once in a while a dinner I don't have to cook, the look of pride my kids have on their face when they conquer new territory, watching people I mentor grow, and taking walks.

I really like walks when the fall leaves are crunching under my feet, or walking on new snow that puffs out from under my (hiking) boots while frosted air wisps out with each breath, a sting to the cheeks from the cold air. I also love the clack of my bike pedals as I race along the bike trail; all reminding me that I am alive and moving. It all fills me with happiness: paying attention to the senses.

When I lived in the desert, I enjoyed watching the mountains, naming each peak in my mind. In the absence of leaves, I crunched gravel and learned to enjoy that sound. If it newly rained in the desert, I was happiest when I could smell the pungent aroma of creosote permeating the air. The creosote is not my favorite smell, but what it represents; newly washed air, makes me happy.

Friendships can be a cause of great happiness as well as sorrow. The fair weather friend doesn't make me anything but stressed out. In fact, I have often thought about them while I struggle to sleep. Yet the wounds of a good friend, said with love are invaluable, as I've mentioned before. True friends make me happy.

What about birthdays? They can be downright depressing when they do not meet your expectations. Sometimes we think maybe somebody will surprise us with a planned date, a surprise party, or an entire weekend away. Others of us may enjoy receiving a card but not the standard off the shelf pre-populated kind. We are happiest when the one we care about writes their own message. (Of course I really get a kick out of some of the hilarious cards out there my kids will send rubbing in how old I am from their perspective).

Simplicity: living in the moment, and not borrowing trouble. Appreciating what I have and understanding each day is a gift: that brings me happiness! And as listed, if I sleep; even better!

Chapter 51. Weird Dreams

We all have them. I get unbelievably excited when I have a dream because it means at some point I fell asleep.

I am not an expert on dreams so any interpretations I make will simply be sarcastic; a KC-ism interpretation.

I'll list my common dreams, because I'm fairly certain you all experience a version of them.

Naked in the Mall: My version of the "naked dream" goes like this. For some reason I am always in a shopping mall and that is a rarity for me to be in one since I hate shopping. I never seem to find myself inside the stores, but walking through the mall itself, past the kiosks and vendors and in and around center court, the food places, and back around again. Each time I am startled to find that I am naked and I'm horribly ashamed. When looking around, people are staring but no one is offering me any assistance. Thank God they're not laughing at me, so maybe I still look pretty good, right? (Sarcasm there in case you think I'm an ego-maniac). But then again, no one is hitting on me either in this dream. My only emotion is "oh no, oh no, oh no". Never ever does it occur to me to enter a store and buy clothing; (although where would have I put my purse?) I am simply lost in the mall naked; and then I wake up. Phew! This is my interpretation of the naked dream. I don't have enough clothes! Or, I'm overly modest?

The Cheating Partner: Vivid dreams of your partner cheating sound familiar to you? I get them every once in a while and they are pretty much irrational. It could be a dream about some co-worker of my husbands' that I don't even know exists, or somebody we do know that in my dream becomes irresistible to him, or as is typically the case; a faceless person! I prefer the faceless dreams because then I can't become paranoid about any one particular person. For some reason, this cheating husband of mine gives that woman much more elaborate gifts, attention, and dates than I ever receive. The worst part is when I wake up: I wake up angry at my spouse and for no apparent reason really; after all, it was a dream. He gets genuinely upset when I wake him up, tell him my dream, and then add the nugget that I'm mad at him. My interpretation: I must have been subconsciously angry at him when we went to bed, or

I'm insecure. It could be he's just that big of a stud muffin; he can't help himself. I'm laughing at that right now since he is the most humble person I know.

Dead People: If you read my book "The Corn Stalker" you will read about more of these dreams in detail. However, we all know someone who died. For me, I dream about the ones I was closest to. The one I'll talk about here is my mother. She died when I was a teenager and I have a lot of questions in my mind regarding her. Each time I dream about her or another one close to me, it's as if no time has gone by. We have conversations, laugh, and speak just as we would when they alive. Never in my dreams do I ask the questions I'd really like answers to such as; "Was dying scary?" "How did you feel?" "What happened at the moment you died?" "Where do you live now: are you in heaven?" And the grossest one; "You can't see me when I'm doing the nasty can you?" Here's my personal interpretation. I'm not supposed to know or they're not allowed to talk about it. Death is to remain a mystery to me. When I hear about people's near death experiences I always find my ears perking up. I guess they were allowed to speak about it so maybe my interpretation is incorrect. It could just be the desire to have one more conversation. Or maybe I just don't want to forget.

Another repeat dream I have takes place at high school. I'm sure this is pretty common. My dream is that I forgot my gym locker combination. It's never my hallway locker; always my gym one. It somehow is the first day of school and I panic. Irrationally, my school schedule seems to be tied to that locker combination. That's the part where dreams make absolutely no sense; my school schedule should be in my hallway locker with my school books, yes? Inevitably, I find myself in a line at the school office explaining I have no idea how to get into my locker nor do I know where my classes are located. Sometimes I dream only about the class part; I wander the hallways drifting into classrooms hoping I'm in the right class. Sometimes I go an entire semester still wondering if I'm in the right class. How would you interpret this one? Is it Insecurity again? After all I am wandering halls just like I wandered the mall, only with clothes on. Or am I afraid to be forgetful, anxiety ridden for anything new? I'm not sure but those sound like reasonable explanations. If you've had the high school dream then you have already formed your own opinion as to the whys.

I have a friend named Maureen who is a very active woman: she rides a motorcycle, jogs, stays up all night and works all day; a really fun energetic person. So when she sleeps, some of her dreams are understandably pretty active. Here are two of her dreams. In the first one she said she was running down the side of her old Quonset hut church and people were chasing her but as she ran down the sidewalk she got the brilliant idea to play like MacGyver and jump up and grab the awning at the end of the sidewalk and swing herself up out of site! It worked and she saved herself! She said she always watched for an opportunity to use that move in real life - but so far, nothing. I told her that this interpretation is easy: she's extremely active and has some moves still on her bucket list! Sometimes she even dreams a version of this one where she is running in business clothes and high heels.

Her second dream is more sedate. Every time she has a high fever she has the same weird dream. She's lying face down on top of a lush, grassy green hill and gets sucked up into the sky - it happens each and every time she has a fever! I think the interpretation would be that she feels like she's dying; the grass is soothing to her and because she is a religious woman the sky could represent the afterlife.

Speaking of dying, do you ever get that feeling that you were sucked up out of your body as my friend Maureen felt? Sometimes I feel literally airborne and it feels so real: that's the creepy part. (Personally, not into sky diving). Or I'll feel like somebody is holding me down; almost like a hand is on me. No I am not one of those people who believe there are cling-ons in the room waiting to do some kind of exorcist thing on me. My interpretation for the pressure is that maybe I don't feel good. We certainly can blend sounds and sensations into our dream that are really happening; at least I do. If my head hurts when I'm awake, it may be hurting in my dream character, too.

What about the then and now dream; the one where the past and present collide? I often will dream about people from a former compartment of my life; maybe someone I met in another State and they will be a prominent figure in my current life; people who have never met nor heard about each other. For example, when I was in Arizona, I had a girl I worked with who worked with the computer systems in our company and also had a hobby teaching cake decorating. She was excellent at both. In the State I now reside, I have a friend who recently got married. Somehow my Arizona co-worker made the cake for my friend 2000 miles away. I dreamed she even had a shop right next door to the bride's apartment. How convenient is that? I've had versions of then and now all my life. Interpretation: the cake decorator friend is really good so maybe I wanted her to get a jump start by having a business near my current life so I could help her get established?

Dream Travel. There are some people who believe in conscious dreaming. I'm not sure of the technical term; maybe dream surfing? They believe they can travel anywhere they desire in their dreams and because they can control their thought process; their dream life is much more preferable to their real life. Sometimes the dreams can be more frequent and they become the reality. One of the examples that come to mind from the near past was the guy who shot Congresswoman Gabrielle Gifford in Tucson. He lived in dream world so I'm told.

Some dreams I have feel very real; kind of like the feeling I get when reading a good book: I get transported. Now was I really there? Well I don't believe so, but it sure feels real while dreaming and sometimes it's a bummer to wake up before the dream is completed. (Some of you may dream about ex-loves: probably not a good thing to share with your current partner). Interpretation? Sometimes it's just good to get away from what can sometimes be a mundane life.

At other times dreams are just plain strange. (Remember Max The Slovak Ghost?) Here's one that I had recently. I was in high school again but this time there was a conveyor belt type row of floating seats for babies. It resembled what you'd see in an airport baggage claim. The babies were floating down the hallways in these seats. The students rode on escalators but they were rolling escalators that would dip and slide. It felt like a mild roller coaster. I have no real interpretation for this dream other than it was really cool and maybe I place way too much importance on high school! Oh and another thought strikes me; do high schools have day cares now to help single mom's complete their education?

I am not a Sci-Fi fan yet I can dream in the most amazing Sci-Fi scenarios. If I could only remember them it'd be "Harry Potter watch out, because my characters are equally incredible."

Here's my interpretation; I have an over-active imagination! Ha!

The last one I have was told to me by a friend who is struggling emotionally and financially. The interpretation is clear; see if you agree. She was also in a shopping mall, but naked only from the waist up. There was a bridge outside the mall and her 4 little boys were living underneath of it. Somehow she ended up in a windy area at mall center. Money was flying all around and over her. She kept jumping and grasping at the bills just as a contestant would in those money booths with the fans blowing the bills over and around you. She floundered and could not catch a single bill. Just like with my shopping mall dream, she didn't think about getting her nudity covered. My interpretation? I think we can all come to the same interpretation on this one. She feels out of control and is terribly worried.

The last one I'll leave you with is about a pro golf shop. The golf shop sold tennis rackets which is why I was dreaming about it. (I love tennis). While inspecting the various sizes and grips on the rackets, my attention drifted to the other side of the store where an argument had ensued. Ever curious, I wandered over to the golf department to see a discussion between a store patron and the manager. The customer was gesturing toward a sign near the golf clubs that read "teenagers not allowed to purchase golf clubs; ID required." The customer was yelling about the logic behind this sign while the manager was calmly trying to explain that it was like the locks on spray paint cabinets; teens were not always responsible with those items. In this case the customer did not agree with the store's logic that a golf club could be used as a lethal weapon. I woke up after this explanation and tried to puzzle it out. My interpretation was that I was in a political frame of mind and probably watched one crime show too many before going to bed even though I didn't recall any crimes with a golf club. I wonder if the same rule would have applied to Frisbee golf. You could zing one at somebody's head. Really, anything could be a weapon if you wanted it to be.

While you read this, think of some of the outrageous dreams you have had. I find it a good exercise to understand why I dream what I do; it gives me personal insight. I think I've decided I'm either outrageously cuckoo or just as busy in sleep as I am when awake, which leads me to our final chapter: tying up the loose ends.

Bored To Sleep

Chapter 52. Loose Ends-Miscellany

This book was not intended to be read as a novel; it was meant to be a chapter once/week or more often depending on how often you desired to have a short blurb to read in order to reset your mind and help you sleep.

In this last chapter I will ramble one final time. I'll leave a blank page for you in the back to make your own notes; maybe prompt you to write down a funny incident, a dream, or any idea that will not leave you alone.

I still can think of so many things to bore you with. In fact, did you know that when sewing through a loose strap on a backpack it's a good idea to have a thick needle and wear a thimble? A thimble is a metal fingertip with divots on it. The divots allow the head of a needle to slot nicely into their little indention while pushing the needle through thick material. It prevents the user from hurting their fingertip while they push the needle through the fabric. Some people even use thimbles when they sew buttons because their fingertips are so sensitive. I have no idea which finger you're supposed to wear the thimble on, so I try different ones. I do struggle with using them, though, because they feel old fashioned: something my mom used.

I hear that too much stimulation such as computer and television use before bed can have the opposite effect you may have intended; it keeps your brain and eyes over-stimulated. What I do, (and clearly it's not working) is to watch something mindless on television that does not require too much thought.

I have never been one for games, but recently got addicted to "Candy Crush Saga". I have never ever played an electronic game prior to this one. I'm quite simply hyper-active. Yet I find it mesmerizing and undemanding on my brain's faculties. The problem is that I learned cheats for it such as I can take my tablet and set the date and time forward. When I run out of lives I just push time into the future and they all renew. Candy Crush Saga gives you 5 lives that take 30 minutes each to renew. Since I can change time I can go on indefinitely trying to crush the little candies. A cautionary tale here; remember to set your phone or tablet back to the original time if you use these devices as your alarm. Mine is now set 28 days in the future so if you wanted to be literal, my alarm wouldn't go off for 4 weeks and I might just miss a few appointments.

Speaking of being addicted to Candy Crush Saga……..: true story. When we were listening to music under the stars at the custard shop, I was engaged in conversation with my friend MJ. Shortly before we had left home to meet them there I had been playing Candy Crush. Us women; we tend to make eye contact when we speak, unlike our counterparts who look anywhere but at you. While we were talking I found my mind drifting. Not because she's not a great conversationalist, because she is, but because I hadn't purged Candy Crush from my mind. I found myself thinking that her eyes were the shape of some of the candies in the game. I mentally saw myself sliding the right eye over to the left and wondering if it would create a cascade effect down her nose. I kid you not! I realized during my conversation with my friend that I had better wipe the vague look off my face or else she was going to think I wasn't listening. I even glanced at a pillowed headboard yesterday on a commercial and thought those pillows looked like the white blockades in the Candy Crush game and wondered if I could make them crash down with a row of fruit candies.

Bored To Sleep

Evidently it is time to wean myself from that game! I am too easily distracted.

We all have our guilty pleasures such as what television shows we watch and which ones we don't admit to. I'm addicted to the HGTV network (Home and Garden television). It is a station that caters to the do-it-yourselfer, home purchaser, home seller, or garden enthusiast. I love to roll up my sleeves and paint or come up with some money saving idea that will improve the function of our home. I joke that I want a pink toolbox. Many times when I cannot sleep I lie in bed and dream up all sorts of ideas spurred from shows I watched on home décor.

I watch all the true crime shows because my first book is based on crimes that really happened. It's probably not a good idea since these shows can be the last thing I think about before going to sleep.

I love singing competitions. I'm a wanna-be singer, singing into my hairbrush, doing the dance steps, who tells myself if some of the artists who have recorded can sell records, then so can I! And then I wake up!

We are also huge fans of "Survivor", because it is a fascinating study into the human psyche and how to manipulate other people. I am riveted! We have "Survivor" parties where we gather with food and laughter, booing and cheering. I will not admit to watching "The Bachelor"; oh no I won't.

I'll share with you something I continue to learn: Do not nod in a conversation and smile politely when someone is talking about something or someone that you cannot clue in on or follow: you will be quizzed later and look like a really bad listener. The sticking point for me is that when I interrupt and say "now who is that?" that they get offended and tersely reply "My daughter!" Oh silly me! You might remember me mentioning this is an earlier chapter.

I'll give you a bit of miscellany here: Tidbits that might make your life easier and give you one less reason to stay awake with regrets.

When making popcorn on the stove, make sure you put oil in the pan and remember to shake it while the corn pops: it distributes the oil and keeps the corn from burning. Oh, and keep the lid on.

Don't go into business with a family member. It is so much more awkward post-business.

Don't go into business with friends unless they're disposable or you're all super great at getting along and letting go of differences. (I find my husband is better at this than I am: to me it gets personal).

Get a toothpick when you leave the restaurant; lettuce actually does get stuck in the front teeth; either that or don't smile too widely after your meal. Don't use your straw as a toothpick unless you're desperate.

Humidity makes you sweat like a stuffed pig; not a great idea to jog in 100 degree heat index in the Midwest; just saying!

Singers performing on live shows....please have someone hand you a towel when the camera is pointed at the band behind you and wipe those drips off your face; the camera loves those drops and my kids will keep commenting 'ooh gross' if you don't remove it.

When you're stewing on something that just chaps your hide, flip the coin. Dr. Phil once said "no matter how flat a pancake, it always has two sides."

Sleep on anything big (well okay, try to sleep) before committing; such as large purchases or a commitment of your time!

If you have dry itchy skin, (ahem, you know who you are), stop scratching like a bear and use the lotion placed prominently in your bathroom: seriously!

When us women say "it is okay, you don't need to get me anything for my birthday; I just want you", at least buy them a card.

Men do not take women so literally; When I said to my husband this month, I appreciate all the love emails you send me each morning, but it'd be nice to hear you say all those beautiful words, too.

He interpreted it as "don't get her a birthday card or write her a note like she used to love, just say it out loud; Happy Birthday!" Get my code book, all right?

Now that you've learned all about my stupid dreams, pet peeves, how to scout, sew, prevent embarrassing moments, laugh at your employer and spouse, and warm up your vocals, don't you feel enlightened? No more are you alone with your insomnia: there is a whole multitude of us out there.

Yes I know you don't care about all of these stories, but that was the point, wasn't it? You are hopelessly, painfully, and unbearably bored!

In conclusion I have decided this. Insomnia is a gift; gifts to create, write a song, conceive of an invention or change the world. Cheers, fellow insomniacs!

Bored To Sleep

Bored To Sleep

www.ingramcontent.com/pod-product-compliance
Lightning Source LLC
LaVergne TN
LVHW051448080426
835509LV00017B/1704